INVITATION AND RESPONSE

INVITATION
AND
RESPONSE

Essays in Christian Moral Theology

ENDA McDONAGH

SHEED AND WARD · NEW YORK

First published in Ireland 1972 by

Gill and Macmillan Limited
2 Belvedere Place
Dublin 1
and in London through association with the
Macmillan
Group of Publishing Companies

First published in the United States 1972 by

Sheed and Ward, Inc.
64 University Place,
New York, N.Y. 10003

Jacket design: Jim Claffey

Library of Congress Catalog Card Number: 72-6252

ISBN: 0-8362-0504-9

Printing history
5 4 3 2 1

Nihil obstat: Gerardus Mitchell, S.T.D., Censor deputatus.

Imprimatur: +Josephus Cunnane, Archbishop of Tuam. 7 July 1972.

ACKNOWLEDGEMENTS

The publishers wish to thank the following for permission to include copyright
material in this book: Ferdinand Schöningh Verlagsbuchhandlung, West
Germany, for 'The Natural Law and the Law of Christ' from *Ius Sacrum.
Klaus Mörsdorf zum 60. Geburtstag,* edited by Audomar Scheuermann and
Georg May; Palm Publishers Ltd., Canada, for 'The Christian Ethic—a
Community Ethic' from *Theology of Renewal,* vol. II, edited by L. K. Shook;
and Verlag Herder and Co. Gmbh., West Germany, for 'The Declaration on
Religious Freedom', from *Volk Gottes,* edited by R. Bäumer and H. Dolch.

Printed and bound in the Republic of Ireland by
Cahill & Co Limited Dublin 8

Contents

Introduction

THE developments which have taken place over the past fifteen years in the discipline known as 'moral theology' within the Roman Catholic Church are at least so far-reaching as to make the manuals in near-universal use even ten years ago almost entirely irrelevant now. These developments affected particularly the basic approach to morality for the Christian, although naturally particular problems had to be rethought in the light of the new basic approach. And indeed several problems hitherto regarded as outside the field of interest of the moral theologian had to be confronted by him.

All this proved exciting but confusing for the teacher and student of moral theology in so far as these two could be adequately distinguished in a period of such intense development. As a teacher and student for twelve years I have experienced the excitement and the confusion at first hand. How I found my own way through the confusion, obviously in close dependence on my fellow-theologians, teacher and student, will be indicated in the collection of essays published here. While they are for the most part occasional pieces and many of them can be found scattered through a dozen publications, it seemed useful to collect them together here as an aid to those who find the range and diversity of the literature so great that they do not recognise any uniformity of approach either at basic level of the meaning and framework of morality for the Christian or at the level of particular application in various fields.

My own primary interest has been 'basic approach' in a course of 'fundamental moral theology'. In pursuing this interest I realised the need to integrate moral theology closely with the other branches of theology, especially Scripture and dogmatic theology. More than half the essays are concerned then with the basic approach and the scriptural and dogmatic background as revealed for example in the covenant structure of morality as centred on Jesus Christ, the centrality of charity, the relation between 'nature' and 'grace', morality and prayer. However attractive such a basic approach may be, its final criterion of validity is in the light it throws on particular areas of human behaviour, and a number of particular applications are included.

Theology today perhaps more than previously has an inescapably autobiographical quality. What a theologian produces depends on the demands made upon him in the course of his erratic history and on the resources he can command to meet these demands. In retrospect he sees how limiting both these must be. Yet without the limitation of particular demands it is hard to see how he would produce any real theology at all. His own limited resources operating within the context of theological community and the wider believing community enable him to make his own small contribution to the growing understanding to which these communities are committed.

There are further important lessons here for the theologian. He clearly has no monopoly of truth and even in a relatively confined area he cannot claim to have discovered the only valid or even the best approach. If he does favour one approach over another, and he may have good reasons or even find it necessary to do so, he should be mindful of the possibility of other approaches and he should be able to appreciate them. The pluralism in theology which is often advocated for the good of the Church should be reflected in the individual theologian who should be able to take a quite different point of view from his own and approach his problems from it. Otherwise he is likely to become the slave rather than the master of his approach and begin to fit reality into it, procrustean fashion.

In this spirit any theologian will be very conscious of his debt to and continuing dependence on other theologians and the wider believing and intellectual communities. In the complexities of today the moral theologian depends closely as already indicated on the specialists in other fields of theology, in Scripture, dogmatic theology, history of theology; he also depends for his understanding of the human dimension of his discipline on the natural and human sciences, from physics and biology through psychology, sociology and anthropology to the philosophical analyses and reflections which touch on the understanding of human behaviour. He can function only as part of a team but there is no easy way to defining and confining his team-mates.

If the discipline really does live, it will continue to change and so will its practitioner, the moral theologian. Some of this change will be evident in the essays here even though the same basic approach persists. In the last couple of years I have been attempting to take a different starting point and basic approach from the one which dominates here. How profound and far-reaching the difference is I am by no means sure. At the same time I have become more than ever convinced that the basic approach offered here has a continuing validity and may be much more helpful and appealing to many Christians, with its explicit Christian and biblical starting point, than my more recent attempts to develop a theology of morality based on immediate personal experience of the moral call as a human phenomenon. The two approaches might be seen as complementary rather than conflicting if the reader is interested enough to examine both in this and a projected second volume.

I

The Study of Christian Theology

A Personal Study

Christian theology is a revealed theology, a theology which investigates God's self-communication to man at the person-to-person, revelation level. The communication or revelation became concrete and perceptible in a series of historical interventions which reached their climax in Jesus Christ, whence the title: Christian theology. Having recognised God as addressing man in and through Christ, Christian theology explores from within that communication as the way to a true understanding of God and so of man, and then as a guide to how man should live. 'And this is eternal life [i.e. the only finally and permanently valid life for man] that they may know thee, the only true God and Jesus Christ whom thou has sent' (*John* 17:3).

In any particular form of study it is not genuinely scientific to impose a method borrowed from other studies where it has proved useful. It is not scientific to apply the methods of physics or mathematics to literature or history. It is not true scholarship to classify and interpret ancient literature or ancient writing of history according to modern categories. On the basis of commitment to the truth and of the acceptance of the general laws of reasoning and verification, a scientific investigator finds that the specific methods of investigation vary enormously from science to science and are really imposed by the precise scientific matter investigated. This applies to theology as much as to history, physics or psychology.

In theology, by definition, the precise matter to be investigated is God: in revealed theology it is God as he has revealed or communicated himself personally to man; and in Christian theology it is God as he has revealed himself in that history which came to a point in Christ. To investigate or to study God as he reveals himself in this way, it is necessary to recognise him in the revealing. Such recognition, elementary and primitive though it be, is called faith. Theology then is an attempt to explore the object of faith, the God who manifests himself above all in Christ and is recognised as such. Properly speaking then theology is an activity of faith. *Fides quaerens intellectum,* faith seeking understanding, is an old description of it. Only the believer, he who recognises God in the act of self-disclosure called revelation, can be a theologian.

Theology then is not an impersonal examination of external phenomena but a personal exploration of a reality internal to the explorer, a personal relationship. The divine revelation cannot be reduced to an impersonal communiqué. It takes the form of a personal relationship initiated by God with man. What God communicates or gives in revelation is primarily himself. By speaking to man out of himself God enters this person-to-person relationship. It is only in this relationship that he can be understood, that his self-communication can be systematically investigated, that theology is possible. Without such a recognition of the personally communicating God, however vague and unformed it may be, the exercise of theology cannot begin. The matter of theology determines the manner at least to this extent.

Such an 'insider' approach to theology has its dangers. But it does not necessarily make the theologian a 'sucker', dishonest or infallible. The more extensive protection which by the nature of Christian theology he has against these dangers will emerge later. It is clear, however, that the attempt to study a personal relationship from within, which is finally the only way it can be studied, does not inevitably involve the person studying it in self-deception. There is a genuine reality here which he can experience and understand more fully although he will have a series of other relationships as well as other people's recorded experience to help him to interpret this particular one of his own. But the danger of self-deception is there and is recognised to be there so that he cannot argue from any personal infallibility about his understanding of the relationship, still less about his understanding of the other person in the relationship. It is only a person with whom such a relationship exists that one can hope to understand in a genuine way. The limits of this understanding are painfully obvious. Again the temptation to dishonesty in face of suspected or discovered mistake is serious but not irresistible. It subtly urges us to form the other term of the relationship according to our own desires, acknowledged or unacknowledged as they may be. It is the besetting temptation of people, clerical and lay, to turn the God of revelation into a God of their own making. Their sins have taken the religious failures of mankind along this way of idolatry, substituting for the one true God who has spoken to man some other god more immediately satisfying to particular human needs of power or money or sexual satisfaction. The failures of Israel have been typically described as such idolatry, the creation and worship of idols. The Jews of Jesus' time, and above all their religious leaders who earned his only harsh words, made exactly this mistake. The God they worshipped in their meticulous observance of the law, in their confusion of the essential and accidental, was no longer the true God of Abraham or Isaac or Moses but such a distortion of that true God that they could not recognise him as speaking to them in the person of Jesus Christ. Explicit affirmation of belief or scrupulous execution of external worship is no guarantee against serious self-deception and dishonesty, against total failure to recognise the one true God. The vocation of the theologian demands constant vigilance against such idolatry as he seeks to attain for others as well as for himself some of that fuller understanding of the God of Jesus Christ which constitutes eternal life.

While theology is the attempt to understand from within the personal relationship between God and man or rather God as he manifests himself in that relationship, it bases itself on certain historical data. The self-manifestation of God is made concrete in the history of the people of Israel and of Jesus Christ and his Church. It further accepts and allots a place to the whole of the physical universe and to the totality of human experience and history. Clearly then the study of historical elements of revelation as well as of the history of cosmic and human origins carried out on their own terms, with the manner determined by the matter, will have a role in the proper development of theology. The scientific evidence for evolution, the valid conclusions of the study of history and literature contemporary with those of Israel, the historical study of the Judaism of Jesus' time, the developments in psychology and sociology, all these and many other sciences contribute to the theologian's understanding of the true nature of the God-man relationship. They are not of course studied first of all in the light of faith or for the sake of theology but for their own sakes, for the sake of the truth. Their true findings then help theology in its quest of faith.

Similarly the historical and literary study of the revealed religion of Jesus and his predecessors has many aspects to it that do not immediately involve faith. Such studies are necessary for any effective theologising but only by being integrated into or vitalised by a living faith do they become genuine theology. The studies of Christianity, its origins and development, by honest 'outsiders' can be of immense help to the 'insiders' and should be warmly welcomed for this, and carefully examined for the new knowledge they bring as well as for the misunderstandings they may involve.

Christian theology is also enriched by the insights of non-Christian religious thought, philosophy and literature. Any true understanding of man is an understanding of him in his actual situation. In the world of his own time he is addressed by God in the person of Jesus Christ. Men sensitive to the depths of the human personality, its capacities and needs, its successes and failures, its hopes and despairs, are not necessarily professing Christians. It is quite obvious that today (as perhaps always) most of them are not. Yet their grasp of the human condition is very important to theology, not only that it may be relevant to the men of our time but that it may be true to itself as the study of the God-man relationship today.

The relative value of Aristotle or Sophocles, Buddha or Mahomet, Kant or Shakespeare, Marx, Darwin or Freud, Gandhi or Pasternak, for theological understanding cannot be easily assessed. Yet there can be no doubt that these classical writers and thinkers who have contributed so much to man's self-understanding have thereby enriched Christian theology. There is at least an implicit, anonymous theology (to adopt the jargon of the moment) in every serious consideration of man as he is. And the goal of theology even in human terms is not information, however detailed, accurate and organised—but understanding, the full human understanding of man's condition as this created spiritual-material, emotional, social, historical, sexual etc. being who is the recipient of God's self-communication and partner in the personal relationship initiated by that communication. This complete understanding of man is only possible through the understanding of the God to whom he must relate, positively or negatively, explicitly or implicitly. And the understanding of God depends in turn on understanding the man to whom he relates and in whose concepts and terms this relationship must be expressed. For the Christian anthropology (understanding of man) and theology (understanding of God) are two sides of the same coin. And both in their developed state should issue in wisdom.

Ideally the theologian should be a wise man, the wise man a theologian. The scholarship and intellectual analysis which the theologian applies to the word (communication) of God should lead to a fuller understanding of the human condition and the demands it imposes. This understanding is for living. It is wisdom, although in its content it may contradict flatly the worldly wisdom of the day. Theological understanding then seeks expression in human living. It is in its turn dependent on human living. Such understanding comes not only or even primarily to the scholarly, but to the experienced and the good. Scholarship and analysis are necessary ingredients in the development of man's understanding of God and of himself, but the reflecting man of experience, Christian experience, has to confront his own Christian living. The quality of that living affects his scholarship and analysis. It influences his work as a theologian both in its matter—the Christian faith which he is investigating—and in its form—the faith activity which constitutes that investigation. The theologian should be not only wise but also holy. For most this is a call rather than an achievement.

A Community Study

As a consequence of its character as a study of God as he has communicated himself to men above all in Jesus Christ, theology has been described as a personal 'insider' study by one who recognises God speaking in this way, the man of faith. This personal dimension of theology can only be understood in the context of its community dimension. Theology like all study has a community dimension. Man progresses in knowledge through exchange with other men. This applies to all branches of knowledge, however esoteric, in some degree. To seek knowledge at all man must acquire a language, some elementary rules of reasoning and composition and, depending on the particular branch, a greater or less familiarity with previous achievement and present endeavour in that branch of knowledge. Today the dependence of individual biologists, physicists and other positive scientists and even of artists, musicians and literateurs on the 'biology', 'physics', 'art' or other professional community, is widely recognised. And the pioneer or genius, however original he may appear, always shows the influence of the particular community which produced him and depends on the stimulus, criticism and eventually on the acceptance of his professional colleagues. The individual breakthrough realises its true potential when it becomes a community possession.

As a professional study, theology shares the community characteristics of all such studies. It develops from previous achievement through exchange, criticism and acceptance or rejection. The community of theologians has a similar task to that of other professional or scientific communities in promoting knowledge and understanding of its own particular subject matter.

The community dimension of theological study, however, has its own particular character arising from this subject matter. The subject matter, God as he communicates himself to man primarily in Christ, is to be discovered and studied within a particular community. In the Christian dispensation God communicated himself to communities. And the outstanding individuals with whom he came in more immediate contact in the preparatory stage, such as Abraham, Moses and the prophets, had all a community role. The self-revelation of God was always directed to a community and could only be understood and lived in community. The community in turn was created and developed by the self-manifesting presence of God.

In the climactic stage of the divine communication, that communication was incorporated in a new community which would be the visible, historical continuance of the full, proper and permanent incorporation of the divine in the world, Jesus Christ. It is within this community that the individual comes into full, explicit contact with God as he communicates himself to man, because it is within this community that man comes in contact with Christ. It is within this community that man lives and explores the faith. The permanent life-giving and truth-guaranteeing presence of Christ in the Church, as this community is called, inevitably conditions this exploration. The final criterion of the correctness of theological development is not acceptance by the community of professional theologians but acceptance in the community of Christians. It is the faith and understanding of the whole Christ that is important and in discerning it all Christians have a role—the general body of believers, the professional theologians and as the finally decisive voice, the college of bishops with the pope at its head. Community decisions at this level have a special role in theology.

The full community dimension of Christian theology then can only be understood in accordance with the peculiar character of theology, as a study of God's self-revelation incorporated in Christ and now accessible in that community of the Church also called the body of Christ.

The personal and community aspects of theology complement each other very closely. Theology is personal in that it is an 'insider' attempt to understand the God of Jesus Christ as he communicates himself by one who personally recognises and accepts that communication. But one does that within the community where Christ is present, presented, preached. Indeed it is becoming increasingly evident that person and community are in general correlative terms. One can only become a human person within a human community and the interchange between individual persons and community is the source of development for both. The believing person finds his faith, his first recognition of God speaking to him in community, the family or local or school community but ultimately the Christian community. And he develops his understanding of God within that community and so in turn contributes to the fuller community understanding. Theology will always be both a personal and a community task.

A Biblical Study

God's self-communication to man can be and is described as the word of God. This was a favourite expression in the Old Testament, preparatory stage: 'And the word of God came to the prophet—.' In the New Testament the word of God acquired a much deeper significance. The supreme communication of God to man was of course his Son becoming man. For St John this was expressed by saying 'the Word was made flesh'. And it is this incarnate Word of God (*Theou logos* is the very expression in theology) which is the subject matter of Christian theology as it was this Word of God, the crucified and risen Christ, Christ the Lord, which the community of his disciples was commissioned to preach to all men.

The incarnate Word of God, the preached Word of God—the next obvious stage is the written Word of God. It was a stage which had emerged very early in the history of God's people, when it was yet in its preparatory phase as the people of Israel. And certain written documents had acquired a decisive authority in the community as God's word, an authority recognised during his earthly life by Jesus Christ himself and accepted by his community, the new Israel. However, within that new community written documents also appeared recording the life, message and living demands of the incarnate Word as experienced and preached by the people of his choice and training. Certain of these documents were accepted by the community as having special authority. They were described as the writings of the New Testament or covenant and together with the writings of the Old Testament or covenant they formed *The Book* or the Bible. These writings were recognised as authoritative or normative as providing the standard account of God's revelation by which all other accounts must be measured. They were sacred because they dealt with the sacred relationship between God and man—sacred or saving history—but above all because their very composition was due to a special impulse and guidance of God in his Holy Spirit which has been traditionally called inspiration. As the divinely inspired and divinely authorised account of the communication or Word of God in its primary and fullest sense i.e. the Son of God made man, the Bible is also aptly called the (written) word of God and provides the primary written source within the Christian community for understanding and exploring God as he reveals himself.

The Bible, and in particular the New Testament, is at once a community product and so in some sense secondary or subordinate to the community, and a special divine product enjoying a normative authority which the community must recognise. The community must remain faithful to the Bible. It cannot modify or omit any of its genuine teaching. And yet the Bible can be read and understood only within the believing community from which it came and which together with the written word of God as a distinct feature of itself continues the teaching and vivifying presence of the incarnate Word in the world.

Today more than ever before the Bible is seen as the basis of all theological study. The theologian must be a man of the Bible in order to understand his faith. The various studies devoted to the language, composition and meaning of the biblical documents form an essential part of theology. As a community study of God in his revelation theology will always be seeking a fuller understanding of the Bible as *the* community book, the book of God's people, in which God's word received its definitive written expression.

Rooted in the World

Yet a study of the Bible in the terms and categories of the Bible, what might be called biblical theology, does not constitute a complete theology, a complete *intellectus fidei* (understanding of the faith) for the man of this or any other time. The Bible may never be wrenched from its community context in the Church and studied in and for itself alone. Any kind of biblicism, isolated Bible study, is false to the character of the Christian revelation. And there is a long history (two thousand years) of community reflection on that revelation and on its biblical expression, and of community decisions authoritatively, and occasionally irreversibly, expounding the true meaning of the revelation. A complete theology must incorporate the historical community reflection and authoritative decisions. Only in this way is full value given to the revealed, incarnate Word of God.

While avoiding the danger of biblicism, theology might easily fall into that of ecclesiasticism whereby the Bible and community or ecclesiastical (ecclesial) reflection and decision would be its sole concern. The Word was given to all men. In order to be properly accessible and intelligible to man, the Word of God became man, took on a human nature. To understand the Word of God it is necessary to understand man. In exploring the God-man relationship the developing knowledge and the developing nature of man are important. In promoting the understanding of this relationship amongst men at any particular time, it is necessary to understand the men of that time, to formulate their questions, to speak their language. The theologian must be a man of his time. He must be immersed not only in the written word of God but also in his world, as the Word of God himself was a man of his time and immersed in his world. The Word of God speaks not to a cosy coterie but to all men, and those who having recognised it would more fully understand it, understand it authentically as men of a particular age and culture for that age and culture. The Word was made flesh, human for mankind. The Church exists for mankind. Theology is an activity of the Church seeking to elucidate the meaning of the Word to mankind. To do this it must be true not only to the Word but also to the genuine understanding of humanity proper to its time.

For theology then the historical developments and contemporary findings of many sciences are relevant. And scientific discoveries in physics, biology and psychology as well as the philosophical insights and the conclusions of historical studies have played an enormous role in theological development. From the interpretations or theologising of the inspired writers themselves through the patristic and medieval periods down to modern times, theology and doctrinal expression show the necessary and marked influence of the world of their time. The influence of the Neoplatonists on the early Fathers, of Aristotle on many of the scholastics, and of the existentialist philosophers on contemporary theologians are obvious examples of how theology has recognised the need to be intelligible to the intellectual circles of its day and at the same time profited from the insights developed in these circles. The questions posed to the accepted understanding of the Christian message by the discoveries and theories of Galileo, Darwin and Freud for example, provide convincing evidence of how the development of the positive sciences influences the Christian understanding of revelation. In a similar fashion the archaeological discoveries of the last hundred years and the increased knowledge of ancient oriental religions and religious literature opened the way to a new understanding of how the books of the Bible were written and how they should be understood.

A Historical Study

In its endeavour to understand the Word of God addressed to men, Christian theology must recognise its historical dimension. That historical dimension operated in the actual formulation of the written account of God's Word, in the community's continued reflection on that Word, in the community's official and irreversible statements of the meaning of that Word and it must continue to operate both in the questions it asks of God's Word out of the new knowledge of man and the world which it seeks to integrate and in the terms in which it expresses its understanding of the Word.

In its historical character it looks to the past, to the

decisive historical events of the Word made flesh and the subsequent history of the Word in the community. It looks to the present as it seeks to mediate between the Word and the world of the day to which the Word is addressed. It looks to the future because of the inherent dynamism in both the Word and the world, reaching out towards final fulfilment.

This dynamism in the Word is sometimes described as an eschatological tension, a striving towards the last, final stage of God's self-communication. The definitive communication of God to man was reached in the incarnation, death and resurrection (= glorification) of Jesus Christ. But the completion which was achieved in the glorification of Christ has yet to be fully realised in all men and indeed in all creation. St Paul refers to this glorification of the cosmos or creation in the eighth chapter of his letter to the Romans, but the final glorified state of mankind by sharing in the glorified state of Christ is the persistent message of the New Testament and presented as the coming in glory of the Son, or his second coming. To appreciate properly the divine self-communication in Christ one must see it as the realisation and sign of the gradual glorification of man and the world, the Creator gradually taking possession of his creation, the creation gradually coming to share in and be transformed by the glory of its Creator. In the different sections of theology whether of the Church, the sacraments, grace or the moral life, this eschatological tension should always be taken account of.

The dynamism in the world at the level of its unconscious, spontaneous development, is described as evolution. At the conscious, deliberate level it becomes human history. At both these levels, which interact on each other, the thrust towards the future is perceptible but uneven. At the conscious, deliberate level it is constantly threatened by man's endemic weakness, so that progress in mastering the world's resources brings at once increased opportunity for humanising the world and for destroying it. Human history and progress remain ambiguous, and the ambiguity is only properly explained in the light of faith by man's sinfulness.

However, man and the created world have this progressive, dynamic dimension which makes them as much beings of the future as of the past. This is clearly relevant to any interpretation of the God-man or Creator-creation relationship. It must be related to, although it must not be confused with, the dynamic, of-the-future character of the Christ events themselves. Authentic Christian theology recognises its on-the-way character, the tension inherent in the present situation between what is and what-is-to-be.

The Unity of Theology

What began as a simple and apparently unified investigation of faith in Jesus Christ as God's self-communication to man, has become complicated and diversified by many different if complementary aspects, by many distinct if converging streams of thought. A theology which wishes to be biblical and secular, historical, contemporary and eschatological, to incorporate the discoveries and insights of a hundred other very diverse and separate sciences from palaeontology to Freudian psychology, can scarcely have any recognisable shape at all, much less a recognisable unity. Yet one of the constant paper-claims of the theologians is that theology has such a unity. The most famous of these claims (and claimants) is that of St Thomas in the opening question of his *Summa Theologica*.

The unity of theology as of any science must begin from its subject-matter or the God-man relationship. The subject-matter of theology is the divine self-communication to man drawing man into a special relationship with God. And all this was achieved in and through Christ.

The source of unity in theology must be then the unifying figure of Christ, where God and man come together in one person. This applies to the total range of its subject-matter including creation as well as revelation in so far as it is manifestive of God or man and contributes to the understanding of the God-man relationship. It applies to the historical, psychological, physical or cosmic dimensions of reality. Jesus Christ stands not only at the centre of the God-man relationship and its history, salvation-history. He stands at the centre of all history and of all creation. He is the point of it all, through whom and for whom all things were made, who restores all things to the Father. At the divine, human and cosmic levels, in its past, present and future stages, theology is one in Jesus Christ.

The incarnate Word of God provides the unifying subject-matter of theology, and at the same time ensures unity of method through his authoritative direction of the community in which theology is properly studied. The method of theology is that of historical and rational and experiential enquiry conducted subject to the guidance of the Spirit promised by Christ to his Church. In matter and manner theology, despite the apparent variety of its sources and argumentation, retains a basic unity founded in Jesus Christ.

Divisions in Theology

The unity of theology is frequently obscured in extended courses by divisions introduced to help the student. The divisions are necessary if the matter is to be manageable at all. But they must not be allowed to destroy the unifying and clarifying vision of Christ, and so of the Father, which theology exists to serve.

The most obvious divisions are those between biblical studies and doctrinal or systematic theology, and, for Roman Catholics, within systematic theology those between dogmatic and moral theology. Biblical studies, as has been pointed out, form the starting point for theological reflection. Nowadays they have become so specialised that they must be presented in seminary and other courses by experts exclusively devoted to biblical studies, while systematic theology tends to be presented by men who take over their findings and integrate them into the historical and contemporary reflection of the Church and the world. In practice this can lead to a dangerous dichotomy between biblical scholars who regard the biblical basis used by some systematic theologians as simplist or out of date, and systematic theologians who see the biblical scholars as falling into the error of biblicism, isolating the Bible from its true community setting in the Church of today, and treating it as a totally independent entity. The solution to these difficulties calls for greater theological awareness amongst the exegetes and a better biblical formation for the theologians, but it calls above all for very close co-operation in presenting the Christian message. The exegete can never hope in these specialised days to be a complete theologian. The theologian cannot hope to be at the same time a fully-fledged exegete. By merely presenting a scripture course side by side with a systematic course the dangers will not be overcome. The various sections should be worked out together by the scriptural and systematic teachers to give students a unified scriptural and theological understanding of each aspect of the Christian revelation. Some drastic rethinking of the divisions of theological courses may be demanded before this is achieved.

The Emergence of Moral Theology

Within doctrinal or systematic theology itself there is a traditional division into dogmatic and moral theology. It may not be entirely accurate to describe it as a division within doctrinal or systematic theology. For some time only dogmatic theology has been regarded as systematic or doctrinal theology, and moral theology has been seen as something quite separate and closely allied with ecclesiastical or canon law.

The genesis of the division between dogmatic and moral theology and the alliance between moral theology and canon law form an interesting if complex chapter in the history of theology. For St Thomas and the scholastics the division did not exist. His *Summa Theologica,* which affirms in its very first question the unity of theology, sets out to cover the whole range of Christian theology including its moral implications. What has been isolated as the matter of moral theology is dealt with mainly in the Second Part of the *Summa,* but one would be unfaithful to the mind of St Thomas to isolate this as a tract on moral theology. For him all theology was one and must be treated as such.

However, both practical and theoretical developments after St Thomas resulted in courses and manuals of moral theology separated from and scarcely related to the dogmatic theology which studied the great central mysteries of God's self-communication in Christ. If Christian theology is described as the study of the divine self-communication in Christ, it would be difficult to describe this later separated moral theology as Christian theology at all.

The practical impulses which led to this separation have a long history in the Church. A decisive stage was reached with the development of the *Libri Penitentiales* (Penitential Books) which originated in Ireland during the sixth and seventh centuries. These books, closely associated with the rise of private or frequent penance, simply listed for the private confessor sins and the appropriate penances. After the IVth Lateran Council in 1215 when annual confession became obligatory, a new species of literature emerged. On the example of the Penitential Books, this was designed to help confessors to distinguish sins and assess the penitent's state. The new books went beyond the mere listing of sins into some considerations of principle and of classification. They were known as *Summae Confessariorum* or Summaries for Confessors. It was a more developed and organised version of these *Summae* which issued at the beginning of the seventeenth century in the Manuals or Handbooks of Moral Theology. The Manuals have followed the same basic pattern from 1600 to 1960.

In the meantime other important developments had taken place. The Decree of Gratian in 1140, as the first major collection of the laws of the Church, was the beginning of an era which saw canon law and its study grow in importance in the life of the Church. Naturally these laws had to be taken account of in Christian living, and became increasingly associated with the moral demands of the Christian revelation itself. This became easier in the late scholastic developments of nominalism and voluntarism, which reduced Christian morality to the 'wilful' laws of God as supreme (and arbitrary) legislator. Christian morality and human law were thought of in legal terms and on the same legal model: law is the will of the legislator, pure and simple.

These and other contributory causes ensured that Christian morality would be closely associated with canon law rather than with Christian doctrine, that it would be expressed in legal terms and that in its concept of itself as a guide for confessors, it would concentrate on sins as breaches of the law.

There were other ascetical and spiritual movements in the Church which tempered or complemented this presentation of Christian morality. There were serious attempts at radical renewal, particularly in Germany in the eighteenth and nineteenth centuries. And the neo-scholastic revival at the end of the nineteenth and beginning of the twentieth centuries gave more body to the rational argumentation and modified the voluntarist influence. The manuals have remained however, by and large, a combination of rational (Aristotelian) ethics in legal form and canon law. And it is only in this century, particularly in the last thirty years, that their deficiencies have begun to be fully recognised and more successful attempts made to replace them.

The Present Renewal

The pioneer in this field was providentially the Bonn Scripture scholar, Fritz Tillmann, in the 1930s. Moral theology's greatest need was a return to its scriptural basis leading to its reintegration with genuine theology. Later work by Scripture scholars such as Rudolf Schnackenburg and Ceslaus Spicq deepened and confirmed the work of Tillman. In the meantime attempts at a systematic presentation of moral theology based on Scripture and closely associated with the central Christian truths have appeared. Of these, *The Law of Christ* by Bernard Häring, an attempt at a new-style manual, and *The Primacy of Charity in Moral Theology* by Gerard Gillemann are perhaps the most significant. But there is now a whole literature of renewal in moral theology consisting of both books and articles. And the general tendency is towards a moral theology that seeks to understand the implications for living of the central Christian truths or mysteries.

Despite the volume of literature, the renewal of moral theology has but begun. Some such beginnings were made at other times and in other places. Yet the present start seems much more likely to persist. It may be worth reflecting why it should have begun just now and why it seems likely to succeed.

The renewed interest and exciting development in biblical studies have undoubtedly affected moral theologians as they have all theologians. Despite the legal form and the association with canon law, moral theology always kept some vestiges of its biblical origins. The explosive energy of the biblical movement was bound to affect it in a radical way.

The other movements in the Church, theological, liturgical, and ecumenical (in so far as one should make such divisions) created a new context of Christian reflection into which much of the legal formulation, rational argument and negative attitude of the manuals fitted uneasily. The developments in the theology of the Church, for instance, from the previous emphasis on a juridical organisation to greater preoccupation with the internal life of the Church as the Body of Christ and its character as God's people, a community of freed and free people, have enormous implications for the behaviour of the individual Christian with which moral theology traditionally concerned itself. The Constitution of Vatican II on the Church officially recognises, by implication at least, a new stage, the theology of Christian living.

Similarly, the liturgical movement, in its efforts to awaken Christians to their role as active participants in the worshipping response of Christ to the Father, has underlined the unified, Christian and response character of all human living. The liturgical or worshipping community of Christians must also be the living and serving community of Christians. The source of Christian moral behaviour is Jesus the Christ, the Lord of the eucharistic community, Lord of history and Lord of creation. The parallel developments in the theology of the sacraments seen as personal meetings with Christ, have revealed the invitation-response character of these and their need to be integrated with daily living and all human activity.

A further fertile influence has undoubtedly been that of the ecumenical movement. Both as a challenge and as a guide, the attitudes of the Reformed Churches to Christian morality are helpful. Their criticism of much of Roman Catholic moral theology as too legal in its approach and too divorced from Scripture must be accepted as to a large extent justified. The more biblical, Christ-centred and charity-inspired presentation of some theologians in the Reformed tradition provides a useful pointer for Roman Catholics, while their inconsistency in theory and frequent confusion in practice is a warning about the dangers of such an approach.

In philosophy and psychology as well as theology the insights of the day stress the value of the individual person, his need to mature through responsible, free activity and his commitment to the community. So the movement to renew moral theology for all its limited beginning seems destined to grow in the coming decades, and may perhaps later be synthesised within the totality and unity of theology in a way comparable to that of St Thomas in his day.

It is not possible, however, to hang outside any department of theology, least of all that dealing with human behaviour, a notice saying: 'Closed for reconstruction.' Business must go on as usual because Christian living has to go on as usual. And so it is with any attempt to outline the basic structure of such Christian living. All the time one is aware of the background noise of bulldozers demolishing the solid walls which formerly clothed the structure, aware too of the dangers of falling masonry for the guide and the guided, of how the combination of old and new styles may conflict sharply and confuse, of how shoddy material may be slipped into the reconstruction or looters may filch some of the authentic structure. Yet the basic structure is, I believe, sufficiently solid to stand the necessary reconstruction and sufficiently defined in shape to appear clearly through the confusion necessarily associated with reconstruction.

2

The Natural Law and the Law of Christ

IN THE present task of theological renewal, moral theology is perhaps the section of Catholic theology which is in need of the most sweeping reform. The full extent of that reform or its causes cannot be discussed here. This chapter is confined to one central aspect of moral theology as it has been presented in the Catholic tradition, the relation between *natural law* and *revealed morality* and the legal expression of both. It will examine this relationship in the light of the basic source of all Christian theology, the revelation of Yahweh which reached its culmination in Jesus Christ and it will seek to derive some alternative understanding of moral theology and organisation of it, to that given in the manuals and in some versions of renewal.

The title of this chapter obviously refers to the constituent elements of the manuals of moral theology as we have known them. They were for the most part composed of natural law, commands and prohibitions, plus divine positive laws based on revelation (with a generous measure of purely human canon law). The principle of unity was understood in an extrinsic fashion as the will of God, conceived as a law. The far-reaching effects of all this I have discussed elsewhere.[1] Here two points are relevant: the tenuous connection between such moral theology and the revelation made in Christ and the predominantly legal form in which morality is conceived and expounded. To evaluate this approach in the elements which compose it and the form in which it is presented, it is necessary to turn to revelation as source.

I

In studying the Judaeo-Christian revelation as source of morality, the theologian discovers that what is of first importance is not the explicit moral directives contained therein but the framework in which they are set, the very *structure of revelation itself*. This structure emerges clearly in the Old and New Testament revelations and may be described as a *covenant* (*berith, diatheke, testamentum*) structure in accordance with the predominant description of the revelation. In this structure God reveals himself by entering into a relationship with Israel (mankind), whereby Israel belongs to him in a special way, enjoys his special favour but must respond to this divine initiative in its way of life. God's self-revelation is in fact a self-giving which demands a human *response* which is also a self-giving. Moral theology studies the human response demanded in the light of the divine self-giving. Divine revelation is seen as invitation demanding response, as gift and task (*donum et mandatum, Gabe und Aufgabe*), as announcement of God's favour or salvation, and instruction about the realisation of that favour in one's life (*kerygma* and *didache*). And while all this is veri-fied of the various stages of the Old Testament revelation to the first Israel, it emerges in its full force in the New Testament or covenant achieved in the person, life, death and glorification of Jesus Christ, founder of the New Israel.[2] It is only in this context and with this structure that it is possible to have a Christian moral theology at all.

The task of moral theology then is not to study the 'law of God' but that divine self-giving we call revelation as a way of life for man. In the central exchange between God and man in the Old Testament revelation, the Mosaic covenant, the law for all, in its legal form appears as the way of *response* appropriate to God's people in consequence of his choice of them. It is this choice and the activity in which it has been so clearly expressed which is the basis of the obligations of the people, and the source of their capacity to fulfil them. When this gift-aspect of the covenant and the response it demands are forgotten, and the material demands are treated as a way of establishing in human fashion a claim against God, the Mosaic Law becomes, in the Pauline image, sin instead of grace or gift.[3]

This distortion of his gifts did not prevent God from completing his planned self-giving by sending his own Son. With the event of *Jesus Christ*, the self-revealing and self-giving of God to man reached its ultimate point. God himself became man. In Jesus Christ the relationship between God and man attained its fullest depth by sharing the divine sonship, and its widest range as offered to all men. In him the divine gift and the human response reached their climax. Through him and only through him, God the Father comes to man and the man comes to the Father. As a study in the way of life manifest in the New Covenant, moral theology is centred on Christ. He is the Way. The human activity appropriate to man in his life or in any individual situation of it must be a response of one called to be a son of the Father after the manner and by power of Christ. Jesus Christ constitutes in his totality the norm or standard of good activity in the present order. He is, if we wish to use the expression, the moral law.

This could be developed in more systematic fashion by analysing the teaching of Ephesians 1:9–10; Colossians 1:15–20, the Logos doctrine of St John, and the New Testament preoccupation with Christ as the one mediator between God and man. He is the centre not only of redemption but also of creation.

It could be traced in a more elementary fashion in his *call and instruction of his disciples*. They are not called just to learn from him as from other rabbis. They must share his attitudes and imitate his actions. Eventually they must *share his life* and destiny in a way that had no human parallels. It was an internal, transforming share as branches of the vine or organs of the human body. The life which should issue in their activity was in Paul's insistent phrase, *life in Christ*. And this could be expressed in terms of some participation in the divine being. Through the gift of the Spirit they had become brothers and co-heirs with Christ as sons of the Father. In their lives as a whole and in each individual moral situation, they were faced with an invitation from the Father to which they might only respond as sons.

The being which must now decide their moral activity (according to the axiom: *actio sequitur esse*) was the being of the incarnate Son of God which they had been called to share (*esse filii incarnati*). Without wishing to deny the necessity of describing moral realities in such ontological terms, it is well to be aware of the dangers involved, e.g. misunderstanding our own terms and restricting *esse* in such a way that it regards history as an external and accidental category of reality, or extending the being too far to include, for example, biological elements in an undifferentiated way.[4] And for many people outside the scholastic metaphysical tradition, the axiom makes no moral sense whatever. In discussing the further characteristics of the morality revealed in Christ, this axiom will not therefore be much in evidence.

Given this underlying structure of God's self-giving in Christ demanding human response in Christ, Christian morality might be explored and expounded in various ways. For our purposes it will be sufficient to draw attention to some characteristic aspects of it, which have to be taken into account, whatever particular way or model is used.

The most obvious of these has already been stressed—its character as *gift or grace*. It is solely the initiative of God which is responsible for this covenant relationship. It is his gift of himself in Christ which calls for man's response and enables man to make it. Every moral response will have a *thanksgiving or eucharistic character*. Any presentation of morality which contradicts or obscures this basic gift character by setting up or appearing to set up a human claims system, is so far unchristian.

In the context in which it is given the gift is a *reconciling* gift. It restores sinful man to divine favour. The call to response becomes a call to repentance. Man's self-giving to God must take the form of return, *shub, metanoia.* His life-task as well as each individual action will have a penitential element, as he seeks more fully to be freed from entanglements of the sin of the world and of his own personal sin.[5] In responding to the Father in Christ he will find it necessary to die to self in its egoistic desires. He must be crucified with Christ to share the new life and new creation of his resurrection, to share his sonship. God's total gift of self demands man's total gift in return, and that can be achieved only if one is willing to take up the cross and follow Christ. The cross is an inescapable element in the good life of the Christian, in Christian morality.

The reconciling gift establishes man in a special *relationship* with the Father and with his fellowman. As son of the Father he is brother of his fellowman and vice versa. His moral task is the living or expression of these relationships, which are really different aspects of the one relationship. So Christ could sum up the Christian life as *love of God and love of neighbour*, where that means all mankind, including one's enemies. St John pinpoints love of neighbour as test of one's love of God, and St Paul reduces all commandments to love of neighbour. This is not the New Testament's way of emphasising the primacy of love among equals or as one commandment among others.[6] The new commandment of Jesus derives from the new relationship(s) revealed in him. It is the primary articulation of the demands of that relationship. All other moral demands are particular expressions of love as sonship or brotherhood.

The relational love-character of Christian morality must not be understood in any narrow I—Thou, personalist terms. In Christ each man is related to all others. This will achieve an immediately personal expression (in varying degrees) with only a limited number of people. With most people it can be expressed only through different social institutions. The full *community* range of Christian morality can be understood in the context of God's self-giving to mankind. This has always been directed to a people or community. And its purpose has been the establishment of community.[7] The community to be established emerges in the New Testament as the community of all mankind without any distinction of Jew or Gentile, bound or free. The working for the establishment of such community at the individual and institutional level, is clearly implied in the relationship one enjoys in Christ.

The very brief reference to the community dimension of Christian morality possible here leads naturally into its related *historical* dimension. God's self-giving to man-in-community has a history and so necessarily has man's response. It was only in and through the course of human history that the God-man relationship (like any human relationship) could be achieved. Although complicated by man's sin, his historical infidelity, the relationship did progress to the point of Jesus Christ and explicit sharing of the divine sonship with man. And the completion of that sharing lies in the future. It is still promise and *hope*.

At the centre of this historical development stands Jesus Christ. As future Messiah, present Redeemer, and the Lord who is to come, he is the underlying meaning of every stage of that relationship. So he can now be seen to constitute, in varying degrees of realisation and understanding, the *way for all men* at all times to the Father, their standard of behaviour as sons. When the God-man relationship realised in him is understood to include the total man in all his created reality, and Jesus is seen to incorporate this, it is easier to grasp how all men at all times, whatever their explicit relation to formal salvation history, have been included in the scope of that history and have been related to Christ as its centre and Lord. This is not intended to obscure the importance of the explicit relationship without which we could not speak in these terms at all. Nor is it intended to minimise the very real differences in moral understanding, which have always existed and still exist, or to suggest that such moral differences cannot sometimes, perhaps frequently, be justified. On the contrary, it accepts such historical and cultural differences as due not just to human sinfulness (some are), but as part of the historical character of man, part of his divine endowment in fact, and as confirmed and given ultimate meaning in the historical relationship between God and man, which is revealed in Christ.

For the community, historical development in the moral tasks demanded by the relationship to God and to one another and in the understanding of these tasks is indisputable. But this development is no less true of the individual person. It has found expression in the recognition of *growth in moral understanding* and responsibility, through which each person has to pass. It might be extended to a recognition that every moral action is a response from a particular personal and cultural situation and that it is a good response, the response of a son and brother, if it expresses movement towards the Father as he expresses himself in this particular situation, if it expresses growth and development rather than if it stays on one side of a certain line or fulfils a particular legal demand. In spatial terms moral action is not staying in some place (in the 'state of grace'), it is going to some place (towards the Father and the brother). Moral theology and pastoral practice need to take the historical character of the individual moral life much more seriously.

The historical dimension of Christian morality, at the community and personal levels, may not then be taken as meaning simply that this morality has a past, that it has gone through certain stages of development to reach the present definitive stage. In fact it is no less oriented towards the *future* now than at previous stages of development. The Old Testament promise was fulfilled in the New by the revelation of a better promise and of the way to receive it.

The redemption accomplished in Jesus is an earnest of the future available to all men in him. Their path to that future lies in history, in the succession of presents that leads out of the past into the future. The Christian task involves using resources inherited from the past to transform the present and bring closer the final, eschatological fulfilment. Christian morality has an *eschatological character*. It is preparing the future.[8]

This preparation is in virtue of a gift and it is for a gift. It may not be interpreted as a purely human task or achievement, or approached as if an in-this-world realisation of the final kingdom by man were possible. On the other hand one may not evade this task, on the plea of leaving it to God. One may not retreat into a private area of life as the area of moral activity and refuse to take part in the transformation of the world as service to the brother and Father. Man's response to the Father's self-giving must in its totality involve entrusting oneself completely to the God of the future, to God as he emerges in the *unknown and uncontrollable future* into which man has to move. For the individual's final decisive step into that absolute future (which is God), the step he takes at dying, each important moral action in his life should have prepared him as a trusting step into the unknown towards God and his fellowman. This moral activity has as its other dimension a step into the unknown for the community also, but this will be more evident in some decisions and in some people's lives than in others. Yet it may never be entirely absent from any. Personal eschatological fulfilment is to be achieved in and through the community. Any step towards the one fulfilment is a step, however limited, towards the other.

Given the dominating role of Christ in this outline of Christian morality and the age-old tradition of describing morality in terms of law, it is to be expected that the Pauline phrase 'the law of Christ' would be invoked here.[9] St Thomas Aquinas seems concerned with the same reality when he speaks of the *lex nova*.[10] And the tradition which presents morality as a law had obvious and good reason in the obligatory character of moral demands. Yet from what has been already said of the origin and character of Christian morality, the word 'law' cannot be used here in the same sense in which it is used of human law.

St Thomas makes this clear when he points out that the *lex nova* is primarily an *unwritten* law, a law stamped on our being (*lex indita*) by the presence of the Holy Spirit[11] (whereby we cry Abba, Father—*Rom.* 8:15). It is a law *internal* to us, the shape of our divine sonship as it seeks expression in our daily lives with all the characteristics we have already seen. It is not a law imposed on us from the outside as a human law might be. And it is not a detailed code of written law to be found in the Scripture. There is a written or formulated aspect to it. Otherwise it could not be the object of our discussion at all. This written or formulated aspect does not refer primarily to particular commands but to the reality of the gift, relationship etc., which we have to live. However, it is possible and necessary to go further, after the example of Jesus and the apostolic writers, and to formulate commands, ranging from the all-embracing command of charity to much more particular ones such as the prohibition of lying. The more particular such commands become, the more restricted their field of application. It is impossible to prescribe for the living of a relationship, which is what Christian morality is about, by a detailed code. To attempt to do so destroys the relationship as later Judaism discovered. Such formulated demands as are necessary should be kept to a minimum, presented as secondary and derived (although necessary) from the living relationship which they attempt to express. And the creative character of the relationship, by which new and developing responses are recognised and sought out, should never be obscured, as it is in the usual legal presentation of morality.

Legal formulations such as are found in the Old and New Testament are secondary, derivative and approximate. A formulation of very general application cannot give very precise directions for the individual case and the very precise formulation cannot apply to very many situations. The personal creative character of the relationship involved, in which each man has his own vocation, does not allow for more than a recognition of the general structures common to all such relationships (as revealed in Christ), structures which must be realised in each good response.

The formulation of these is necessary to deliberate Christian living and they may take legal form as commandments or prohibitions. In addition, the moral wisdom and experience of the community and of the individual will offer *guidelines* for normal Christian living, which may not be arbitrarily ignored. But the more exact understanding of the general structures, and so the more exact formulation of commands and prohibitions based on them, is a continuing task of the (Christian) community. So, for example, the respect for the life of the neighbour which emerges from the structure of brotherhood has gone through various stages of refinement in regard to self-defence, capital punishment and war. And development is far from complete in each case. More remote guidelines, such as those in regard to property, are more provisional still. It is when one begins with the legal formulation as the primary moral reality that many of the confusions and dilemmas of moral debate arise. For the Christian theologian the legal form should never be the starting point.

One might summarise at this stage by saying: Christian morality, the way of life revealed in Christ, is distinguished primarily by its structure in Christ. It is based on the reconciling gift of sonship whereby all men are called to turn from their self-centred behaviour and to behave as sons of the Father and brothers of one another. It is personal to each man, yet to each man as member of the (human) community. It is universal in its range, but realised in different historical forms. It emerges from God's historic interventions in the past, but deals with the present as it prepares for the eschatological completion of the divine

activity and of the God-man relationship. It urges or obliges
at the very core of man's existence and so may be described in
an analogous way as a law. Its demands need to be formulated, if it is to be lived as response. But these formulations
are limited in value and approximate in meaning. Detailed
legal prescriptions must always be judged in the light of the
basic relationship and may never be substituted for it.

II

All this offers a very different picture from the conventional
manual of moral theology. In particular where does the
treatment of *natural law* which played such a large role
in the manual fit in? The rest of this chapter will be devoted
to the attempt to answer this question.

It may be easier to begin by excluding one commonly
accepted view of the place of natural law in Christian
morality. This view, with its two-storey image of the relation
between nature and grace, regards Christian morality as
composed of the simple *addition* of natural law (applicable to
all men) and divine positive law (applicable to Christians).
In the only existing order, in which all men are called to be
sons of the Father in Christ, no such simple separation and
addition is possible. It presupposes some natural order
separate from the order of grace (and refusal of grace),
which can be isolated and studied as such. And it usually
understands both natural and divine positive law as capable
of adequate, if not complete, expression in legal commands
and prohibitions. They can then be more easily added
together. But all men exist within the one order, subject to,
modified by, reconciled by, and finally judged by, the divine
self-giving in Christ. This is the structure of the situation
within which they must make their moral decisions and
perform their moral actions, however far they are aware
or unaware of this structure. There is *no purely natural order*
which may be the subject of moral experience and reflection
on that experience.

A quite different view emerges if one begins from the single reality which is there—man called to be son and brother in Christ. The key-figure is, of course, the *God-man*. But the point of the Incarnation was not somehow to distort or diminish man in his humanity, but rather to affirm and confirm this worth and dignity. In becoming man, God paid his full respect, as it were, to man's humanity. Theology today is rightly insisting on the genuineness and completeness of this humanity of Jesus. According to the model and by the power of the Incarnation, each of us can become truly a son of the Father and brother of one another in and through our human endowment.

As it is possible to distinguish reflexively between the human and the divine in Jesus Christ (although they were inseparable in reality), it is also possible (and necessary) to distinguish in men called to be sons of God and so modified in their existence, between the *human* and the *divine* (or its modifying effect). The (moral) response, which men must make to this call in their whole lives or in any particular situation, can in its inseparable unity be distinguished at the reflexive level in this conceptual way.[12] It is, if it is a good response, truly and completely the act of a son of the Father and so the expression of this gift of sonship, and at the same time truly and fully a human act. Indeed in the light of the Incarnation it can only be the act of a son (and brother) in so far as it is a fully human act, and (again however unconsciously) a truly human act if it is an act of a son (or brother). The way to sonship and brotherhood in Christ is in and through the human; and fullness of humanity, attainable in history in degrees, must await eschatological completion as sons and brothers.

In so far as the natural law derives from man's *human nature*, as the moral activity appropriate to or demanded by that human nature, it can be found and distinguished within the present order to the extent that that human nature can. There are, however, many conceptual difficulties involved here. Human nature, as it is experienced, is modified by the divine call and its history as we have seen. Secondly, human nature does not appear except in a certain cultural, historical form which is subject to deep change so that it is very difficult to isolate within concrete human nature those features which, as constituting it or pertaining to it at the metaphysical level, might provide a basis for morality, according to the axiom: *actio sequitur esse*.[13] As a result of this difficulty, particular historical realisations have been accepted as part of the metaphysical essence of man or, even worse, particular sub-philosophical categories (e.g. biological) have been confused with it. Finally there is considerable dispute among Catholic theorists about how natural law should be conceived, grounded and formulated, while, of course, it is not for the most part acceptable to Christian moralists outside the Catholic tradition.

In spite of all these very real difficulties a place can be found for natural law in a renewed Catholic version of Christian morality.[14] And this is true no matter which of the two more coherent and influential conceptions of natural law is favoured: that which identifies nature as the human capacity of recognising man's inescapable moral condition—that he is called to do the good and avoid evil (Aquinas)—or that which concentrates on man's metaphysical nature as the basis for good human behaviour (late scholasticism and most subsequent Catholic thinking).[15] That man has such a capacity is presupposed in the God-man dialogue and necessarily persists in it. That he has a metaphysical human nature distinct from the divine and preserved in its humanity is equally presupposed in the dialogue. Without these two realities the dialogue would not be possible at all. In that context the Incarnation provides a guarantee for the reality and integrity of man's humanity, its capacity for moral knowledge and the moral possibilities inherent in it. These may be realised in extremely differing ways in the course of history, but they can never escape certain basic directions without diminishing or destroying that humanity. What these directions are, is very difficult to formulate in a way that will not involve some historical conditioning of man. Yet this does not rule out the value of doing so, or invalidate the notion of a natural law conceived in this way. Briefly then it may be said that natural law, as the absolute, if general, obligation to behave morally, of which man (as man) is aware in view of the general moral possibilities and obligations which derive from his (metaphysical) human nature, is contained and affirmed within the order of Incarnation and Redemption. Natural law does not exist outside or apart from this order.

As the Son of God become man, *Jesus Christ* constitutes the centre of the moral order, incorporating in himself the moral possibilities enshrined in humanity, which taken in abstraction may be described as the natural law. Where in accordance with the Logos theology of St John and the Pauline theology of Colossians and Ephesians, he is seen as the *centre of creation* as well as Redemption, the foundation of natural law morality appears in him in a deeper and fuller light.

Natural law then has its place in a morality centred on Christ. There remain certain difficulties about the very term which call for brief discussion. The word 'natural' as used here may be very misleading for people who normally employ it, in association with law, for the laws of nature, the physical, chemical and biological etc. laws. Indeed some of this confusion has affected theologians themselves, as the recent contraception debate made clear. Taken in the technical, theological sense as opposed to supernatural, it almost inevitably leads to thinking in terms of a two-storey morality as mentioned earlier. The word 'law', if in association with 'natural' it escapes being thought of in physical law sense and is taken as moral law, is in grave danger of being assimilated to the notion of *positive law,* imposed on man by an external lawgiver and in an extrinsic way. It would then become a collection of commands and prohibitions which would be equiparated in practice with human and positive commands and prohibitions. There are too many examples of this in recent moral teaching and practice for the danger to be ignored. And of course such a concept of natural law is quite foreign to the thinking of Aquinas and the best in the natural law tradition. It might be in the interest of that tradition and of the reality it calls natural law, to drop the term altogether.

What matters is that we recognise man's capacity for and awareness of morality, the respect this involves for the basic structures of his being as man, and that all this has been preserved, deepened and may be said to be ultimately founded in the Incarnation. For the moral demands which arise in human experience without reference to the underlying Christian structure, and this occurs for all men much of the time and for the majority (non-Christians) all of the time, it would suffice to speak of *morality*, the moral order, moral obligations or moral values. The qualifications *natural* or *Christian* may be misleading or unacceptable and clarify nothing for the problem at issue. Within the Christian community, in an effort to understand the moral order fully, its foundation in Christ and the consequent characteristics, already discussed, will have an important role. In dialogue with others the foundation and characteristics will always be implicit. They may have to become explicit to demonstrate that we are being faithful to our own basic understanding, not betraying it or cheating by pretending that something accepted in secular morality can be reconciled with, even deepened by, Christianity.

Reflection on the moral order in which we live is a necessary human task. Christians believe that this reflection is carried on in the *order of grace* or God's gift of himself to mankind. So the reflecting subject (person in community) and the reflected-upon-subject (humanity in person and community) are under the enlightening and transforming power of the divine gift. This need not be consciously adverted to in many instances. Sometimes conscious attention to the divine dimension may obscure the human, prevent it from being given its full value or, by the use of religious terms, hinder exact moral analysis. Christians also suffer the consequences of the sin of the world. Non-Christians also enjoy the enlightening power of the Spirit and in some situations, free from such temptations, they may arrive more quickly and surely at a correct moral understanding. Christians must always be aware of their particular temptations and be ready to learn from all. Moral theologians must be ready to accept and integrate the valid moral insights of all men and thereby try to outline a scheme of morality which does justice to all the elements of that order in which man is called to achieve the fullness of his humanity as son of the Father and brother of all men.

Within this structure of morality, centred in Christ, the moral values enshrined in created humanity and discovered in the history of human reflection find their true place. It is misleading however to describe them as natural, or to conceive them as primarily legal in form. The traditional notion of the natural law persists in a genuine way in such an approach to moral theology, but in an important sense it is neither natural nor a law.

3

The Christian Ethic: a Community Ethic

The Problem of a Christian Ethic

What is distinctively Christian in a Christian ethic is the uncovering of the basic structure of human life and activity as a response to the Father in Jesus Christ, who constitutes in himself the criterion of whether a particular life or activity is such a response (and therefore good for man in this order), or not (and therefore bad). And because every man, irrespective of his explicit awareness of this, is so addressed by God, response in Christ is his only way to completion, and Jesus Christ constitutes the one test or norm of morality (of goodness and badness) for the life and activity of every man, either explicitly or implicitly. It is not, therefore, because of the formulated moral teaching of Jesus in the gospels or of the rest of the New Testament or of the historical and developing Christian community that we speak of a distinctively Christian ethic. Such formulations have their importance, and in some instances as in the statements on the primacy of charity, they would be considered as decisive advances in ethical formulation. But they are necessarily secondary to and derivative from the relationship between God and man definitively achieved in Jesus Christ—a reality internal to the human community as a whole, as well as to each member of it.

Different Approaches to the Christian Ethic

This brief outline of what is specifically Christian in a Christian ethic, that it is the living expression in human activity of God's self-gift to man in Jesus Christ or the human response to that gift which is possible only in and through Christ, introduces one further preliminary point for discussion before tackling the theme proper to this essay, the community character of the Christian ethic.

In outlining the basic structure of the Christian ethic as Christian, a number of different ideas or approaches were used. The Christian ethic is an ethic of revelation not primarily in its formulated content but in its character as the response demanded of man by God's self-revelation or self-gift to him. It is an ethic or mandatory way of life that arises from the relationship into which God has entered with man in revelation, and particularly in its climax, Jesus Christ. Given these general characteristics, it would be possible to describe this ethic in various ways, from various angles.

It could well be called an ethic of the kingdom or kingship (sovereignty) of God. The purpose and message of revelation was to establish this kingship in men's hearts, to make this kingdom a reality on earth as it was in heaven. On the basis of this primary formulation of the message by Jesus himself, the distinctively Christian aspect of his ethic could be developed to express and include all human activity as the instrument or vehicle of the growth of this kingship. Such an approach or model with its immediate New Testament background would have much to recommend it also in dealing with the ticklish problem of applying the Christian ethic to all men and activities irrespective of their formal religious adherence and in allowing the progressive, dynamic character of the Christian ethic to appear as it discusses the value of human activity in terms of its contribution to the gradual development of the reign of God in the cosmos, in the human community, and in the individual human being.

The kingship of God approach to the Christian ethic comes very close to the eschatological approach which would view human activity in its relation to the parousia. The tension between what is already achieved for God, mankind, and the cosmos in the glorified Christ, and what is to be the extension of this in its fullness to all men and the cosmos, provides the criterion for judging the goodness and badness of human activity. Whatever expresses the already achieved in Jesus Christ and develops towards the what is to come is a good action, whatever fails to do this is bad.

No less biblical than these and with more immediate links with secular approaches to ethics would be the development of the Christian ethic as an ethic of love or of freedom. And one could list several others such as truth or conversion *(metanoia)*. The summary by Jesus of the whole law and the prophets in the love of God and love of neighbour and the development of this by Paul and John incline many contemporary Christians to describe the ethic of Jesus solely in terms of love, especially as they feel that in this way the real meaning of Jesus can be made intelligible to people who are not Christian. The value of such an approach both theologically and apologetically is undeniable. It arises naturally out of any vision of the Christian ethic as deriving from the God-man relationship, a love relationship based on God's love of man asking for man's love in response. And it closely relates to the theme of this chapter.

Presented as an ethic of freedom or liberation, the Christian ethic emphasises the liberating or saving aspect of God's activity in revelation. It was by his love for man in Jesus Christ that he set man free from his self-imposed slavery to sin, to the law, and to death. The freedom which the glorified Christ enjoys is offered to all men and is slowly achieved by them in their personal history and activity through the power and guidance of the Spirit of freedom given to them. As a way of liberation, which is also a way of integration, the Christian life and ethic could appear relevant and accessible to men of our time.

The approaches or models described here do not exhaust all the possibilities. The purpose of describing them was to stress an important factor sometimes overlooked in present-day discussion of the renewal of moral theology or of the Christian ethic. In the light of the riches of revelation or God's word to man and the complexity of man in his world today, no one approach to the Christian ethic can do complete justice to the God-man relationship and the way of life it involves. At the present stage, for the foreseeable future, and perhaps always, we will need different approaches or models which describe and illuminate this relationship, life, and activity from various angles. Such approaches will not be completely distinct but will overlap and complement each other. Applied to the Christian life as a whole or to particular areas or situations in it, they will by their overlapping and complementing give a better chance of understanding the general or particular demands of this life. For one problem one approach may be more helpful than another, but for deeper understanding of the Catholic ethic the plurality of models offers great advantages.

I. THE CHRISTIAN ETHIC AS GIVEN TO MAN IN COMMUNITY

The model or approach I have chosen to develop in this chapter, then, I do not regard as the only model or as necessarily the best one. Indeed, such comparisons are not very helpful. That the community approach is well founded theologically and particularly relevant today this essay will seek to demonstrate. The initial choice of the theme was certainly influenced by the preoccupation with the notion of community noticeable in theological and secular thinking today. It would be possible to describe the achievement of Vatican II as a development from thinking of the Church primarily as an organisation, a juridically structured group, to thinking of it as a community, a people united above all by bonds of love in Christ. Such a development is more or less perceptible in the key documents of the Council, for instance the Dogmatic Constitution on the Church, where the first chapter deals with the mystery of the Church, its role as the sign of God's presence to man and of the unity of all mankind. This sign is primarily a people, God's people or community who become such a community by God's calling them and their response to him by faith or recognition and trust in him leading to loving union with him and with one another (ch. 2). Admittedly, this people has a particular structure with a special ministry (ch. 3), but a ministry that exists to serve the unity of the people in truth and love. And the people, including the lay people, enjoy a basic equality in dignity and fulfil in their different ways the role of mediating God's presence and call to all men and of showing forth the unity or community of all men (ch. 4). So far from being the impersonal subjects in an organisation hierarchically organised, rationally ordered and juridically directed, the Church appears in this Constitution as a people bound together in Christ by bonds deeper and more personal.

The free commitment and shared responsibility in love and service to God and neighbour of all members of the Church, which the Constitution underlines, is confirmed and developed in other documents. The Constitution on the Sacred Liturgy and the reforms consequent on it dwell on the community dimension of the Church and its liturgical worship. In the liturgy, particularly in the Eucharist, the community is most properly itself. It realises its true character as God's people through communion with its head, Jesus Christ, in his self-giving to the Father. For this the bishop or one of his ordained associates, a priest, is necessary. As leader he enables the community to enter into communion, yet all are actively engaged in what is a truly community activity. So passive assistance at the Eucharist must give way to active and personal participation. In this community celebration not only the local community, the people visibly present, take part, but the whole community of the Church through the power and presence of its head, Jesus Christ, realises and revitalises itself.

In discussing the relations of the Roman Church *ad extra*, with other Christians (Decree of Ecumenism), with men of other religions (Declaration on the Relationship of the Church to non-Christian Religions), and with all men (Declaration on Religious Freedom, Pastoral Constitution on the Church in the Modern World), the community to community relationship with the respect for truth and freedom and the desire for increased unity in love provides a key to understanding the change in perspective as between the conciliar and pre-conciliar statements on these topics.

As theology remains the attempt to interpret the Word of God to his world at any particular time, it is clear that its developments are not born of any ecclesiastical introspection but of the dialectic between the Word and the world. The increased interest in the theology of community has been anticipated and stimulated by philosophical, sociological and political thinking of that wider world to which theologians and Council Fathers also belong. The encyclicals of John xxiii, *Pacem in Terris* and *Mater et Magistra,* as well as those of Paul vi, *Ecclesiam Suam* and *Populorum Progressio,* were particular and profound tributes to the current secular preoccupation at these different levels with man as a community being. It is in this context of theological and secular thinking about community that the theme of Christian morality as a community morality was chosen for discussion.

The Christian ethic is based on God's self-giving to man in Christ where that divine self-giving becomes an invitation to human response. God establishes a relationship with man which becomes the true meaning of man's life, his ultimate fulfilment, and which although given by God must be expressed and achieved in human living. To understand this relationship established in Christ and the ethic it entails, it is necessary to understand that from the beginning God's call to man was addressed to him as community.

The relationship which God sought to establish with man was always with man in community, with a people.

So the individual found himself addressed by God as a member of a community or people. He encountered God in community by being incorporated into God's people. And he had to live out his own relationship with God, make his own response to God, in other words behave morally, in community as a community being. The ethic of revelation or the human response demanded by the divine self-giving, is a community ethic in the basic sense that it is given to or arises for man in community and must be lived by him in community. And this applies to its preparatory stage as realised in the history of the people of Israel as well as to its definitive stage realised in the person of Jesus Christ.

The history of Israel as recorded for us in the books of the Old Testament is the history of Yahweh's dealings with a people, his giving of himself to a people, the response this involved for them, and the actual response they made. The centre and climax of this history is the Sinaitic (Mosaic) covenant. Through the experience of the Exodus the Israelites have been prepared for this new stage in their relationship with Yahweh.

> And Moses went up to God and the Lord called him out of the mountain saying, 'Thus you shall say to the house of Jacob, and tell the people of Israel: You have seen what I did to the Egyptians and how I have borne you on eagles' wings, and brought you to myself. Now, therefore, if you will obey my voice and keep my covenant, you shall be my own possession among all peoples' (*Ex.* 19:3–5).

The covenant involved for the Israelites a commitment to living as God's people as outlined above all in the Decalogue.

> And God spoke all these words, saying,
> 'I am the Lord your God who brought you out of the land of Egypt, out of the house of bondage.
> You shall have no other gods before me.
> You shall not make yourself a graven image . . .

> You shall not take the name of the Lord your God in
>   vain . . .
> Remember the Sabbath day to keep it holy . . .
> Honour your father and your mother . . .
> You shall not kill . . .' (*Ex.* 20:1–17; see also *Deut.* 5:6ff.)

The Decalogue and the wider Mosaic law formed the way
of life of a people covenanted or bound to God by this
special agreement. It arose out of the relationship between
God and his people.

This covenant and this people looked at once backward
to the origins of the people of Israel and of all mankind, and
forward to the fulfilment of Israel and of all mankind. The
Exodus itself was initiated and achieved solely by the power
of Yahweh who identified himself to Moses as the God of
Israel's fathers, the God of Abraham, the God of Isaac, the
God of Jacob (*Ex.* 3:6) who also 'established a covenant
with them'. Seeing their sufferings in Egypt he remembered
his covenant and decided to deliver them.

This covenant with Abraham, Isaac and Jacob was also
with a people of whom they were, like Moses at Sinai, the
representatives (*Gen.* 12ff.) And the sign of the covenant,
circumcision (*Gen.* 17:10; *Acts* 7:8), became the way of
incorporation into the people, the acceptance by the
individual of the people's relationship with God and the
consequent way of life.

Harking back still further, the covenant between Yahweh
and Noah reveals the same structure. God's self-giving is to
man-in-community asking them to live as his people (*Gen.* 8).
And so to the Hebrew understanding of the origins of the
cosmos and mankind, where Yahweh as Creator and Lord
of heaven and earth and of all men established a special
relationship with all men through their first representative.
The disruption of this relationship was the source of all evil
in the world, evil manifested most obviously at the human
level by the divisions between men, husband turning against
wife (Adam and Eve, *Gen.* 3), brother against brother (Cain

and Abel, *Gen.* 4), until 'the earth was corrupt in God's sight and the earth was filled with violence' (*Gen.* 6).

It was only God's persistent care for man that could overcome these divisions. As that care assumed concrete historical shape it became a relationship with a people through their representatives, but this people in turn represented all mankind, as Yahweh made clear to Abraham, Isaac, and Jacob: 'By you all the families of the earth will bless themselves' (*Gen.* 12:3; 26:4; 28:14).

The covenant between God and his people which was the formal expression of the relationship between them was to be an 'everlasting' one (*Gen.* 17:13; *Ex.* 31:16; *Lev.* 24:8). Despite the infidelity of the people, Yahweh remains faithful, renews the covenant, and promises through his prophets a new covenant and a new people which would be the definite expression of his relationship with all mankind on earth (see *Is.* 42:6; *Jer.* 31; *Ezek.* 16: 60).

The new relationship became a fact in the person of Jesus Christ. The divine self-giving to mankind reached its earthly completion when God the Son became man. The human response reached its fullness in the obedient love of Jesus Christ. In him the new covenant was established (*Luke* 22:20; 1 *Cor.* 11:25; *Heb.* 8–12). And it was again to a community, a people, that this covenant was given. As a community in which there was now no distinction between Jew or Greek, slave or free, male or female, the relationship is extended to all men without exception. And it is a relationship with a people, a new people of God, a new Israel. By being baptised into Christ (*Rom.* 6) one becomes a member of the body of Christ (see 1 *Cor.* 12) which constitutes the new people, encounters God the Father by sharing the sonship of Christ and undertakes the way of life appropriate to this community. The whole of the New Testament emphasises the community dimension of Christianity and how one may come to the Father only through the Christ, by becoming a member of Christ, entering into community with him and one's fellow man. As a response to the divine self-giving in Christ the Christian ethic is an inescapably community reality.

The argument so far has based itself on the salvation history approach of God to man, that he approached man in community. But could he in fact have approached man in any other way? To encounter any particular man means to encounter a community, the community which formed this man, of which he is a member. To be human means to belong to some community, to be a product of it and to contribute to it, to share its destiny, its language, and its way of life to some minimal degree. It is to be the centre of a network of human relationships, however few and tenuous they may be. In encountering a human being, then, one encounters all this. In speaking to a particular person, in entering into a relationship with him, it is not possible to isolate him from his community. Even God could not do this. So that he too had to encounter man in community, to speak to him as a community being, to establish a relationship with him in community. The ethic or way of life which derived from this relationship had necessarily, then, a community dimension, based on God's self-giving to man in community.

2. THE CHRISTIAN ETHIC UNDERSTOOD IN COMMUNITY

The second reason why the Christian ethic should be described as a community ethic is that as it is given to and received in community, it can be understood only in community.

All human understanding is community understanding in the sense that the individual can arrive at it only in some community. The process of human understanding depends on learning a language—a community possession—and, at the beginning at least, on receiving from one's immediate familial, local and wider community basic information, ideas and ideals. It is in the growing interchange with the various communities into which he is gradually incorporated

that a man acquires his specialised or professional understanding (of chemistry, for example, by belonging to the
chemistry community) as well as his overall understanding
of life. This understanding is not the predetermined product
of his social environment, however widely that term is
taken. Even in a scientific field, through his assimilation of
what is already available, he can still make a personal
contribution and enrich the community understanding by
some new discovery or insight. In the personal and creative
fields of literature, music or art the personal contribution is
more obvious, although still based on the community
inheritance and education in these fields, and constitutes in
turn a community enrichment. Where a vision of life is
concerned, the person-community dialectic is particularly
intense. The dependence of the person on previous community understanding and his contribution in turn to future
community understanding constitute a rich dialogue. Even
where the accepted community understanding is personally
rejected at one level, this is always done by somebody
developed in community and drawing on broader contemporary community ideas or on earlier historical community
understanding. The philosophical, ethical or religious genius
who makes a genuine breakthrough moves from certain
inherited community ideas to provide a new or deeper
understanding for community.

All this applies to Christian understanding and a Christian
vision of life (Christian ethic) as much as to anything else.
The history of God's approach to man as outlined earlier
confirms this. As God approached man in community, gave
himself to a community, this self-giving and what it involved
for man had always to be understood in community. The
great religious leaders of the Old Testament like Abraham
and Moses were community leaders. It was in the community
as it acquired more concrete shape that through the direction of its kings such as David and Solomon, the liturgical
instruction and activity of its priests, the counsel of its
wisdom writers, and the inspiration of its great prophets

such as Isaiah, Ezechiel and Jeremiah, the individual Israelite came to know the will of Yahweh, the way of life that was expected of him as a member of God's chosen people. The creation and collection of the Old Testament scriptures which formed a norm of the community understanding were, properly speaking, community activities. Indeed, the Bible as a whole is a community book, written in community, by a community, for a community.

So all this applies equally to the New Testament, both as a new covenant or relationship established between God and man in the person of Jesus and as a collection of normative writings about this relationship. They are both community realities and can be understood only in community.

The new people of Israel has its life-giving centre in Jesus Christ and it finally is made a historical, dynamic, teaching community in the world by the gift of the Spirit at Pentecost. It enters the world to bring to it its own understanding of God's self-revelation in Jesus and what it involves for mankind. On the basis of its own experience now brought to mind and more deeply grasped in the light of the Spirit, the Pentecostal community preaches the good news to others and incorporates them into the community of faith, of true recognition and understanding of God and of the way of life this implies. Understanding the Christian way of life is understanding the faith, the faith as it must be lived. And this takes place within the Christian community.

There are a number of factors in this community understanding that should be mentioned here. As an understanding of God in his self-giving, it is for the community first of all a gift from God, an aspect of God's self-giving to man in the form of the enlightening Spirit, whereby we recognise God and call him Father (*Rom.* 8:15f.).

This gift, however, does not destroy man's understanding, but transforms and illuminates it. The implications of revelation can only be progressively understood by the community. Such progressive understanding follows the laws of human understanding as men explore the fuller meaning of the gift that has been given them. The enlightenment of the Spirit, whereby the community receives and maintains its basic recognition of God speaking to men in Christ, does not absolve the community from the human task of seeking to understand this revelation even more fully. This is a community task and so it is a historical task as successive generations of Christians, building on the understanding of their predecessors, try to understand and explain God in his living Word in a way relevant and intelligible to their time.

This process of historical development applies in a particular complex way to understanding *the way of life* which God's self-giving demands. As societies and civilisations change and develop, the problems of living as a Christian change and develop. The questions that faced the first Christians and their first Council about the Gentiles and Jewish observances no longer bother us. Neither do the difficulties Christians encountered as members of the Roman armies. But every civilisation, every society, indeed every generation faces new questions, new problems, new possibilities. Today, the problems and possibilities of common worship with other Christians, of mixed marriages, of living in various pluralist societies, of the bomb, of population, segregation, and so on, have replaced earlier and different problems. They pose new questions to the Christian community and demand new answers, answers in which the basic God-man and man-man relationship revealed in Christ is maintained, and answers which build on and develop the inherited wisdom and reflection of previous generations, but yet new answers for new people with new problems.

It is the task of the whole Christian community to provide these answers by using all the resources of the community. Every member of the community has an obligation to contribute to arriving at these answers in so far as he can. The contribution will vary from person to person and from problem to problem. For some their contribution will be that of immediate living experience, whether it is a matter of social justice, peace and war, sex and marriage. Others will have some special professional competence, as medical men or economists or social workers, which is relevant to a particular problem. Others will be professionally engaged in interpreting the Word of God to the people of a particular place and time as doctrine teachers or theologians or pastors or bishops. The understanding and knowledge of all these has to be co-ordinated as effectively as possible so that the community as a whole may be able to have the best Christian understanding possible at the time.

This kind of co-ordination demands great energy and goodwill on the part of everybody concerned. It also demands certain channels through which the ideas and information may flow. Few enough of these channels exist as yet. And finally, of course, the co-ordination depends on that basic structure given to the community by Christ whereby Peter and the apostles and after them their successors provide a unifying service in the community, articulate authoritatively, and in some instances definitively, the community understanding and pronounce it in genuine continuity with the historic, if developing, understanding of the community established by Jesus Christ and now living in him. To enable the apostolic college to perform this service as well as possible the community as a whole must perform its tasks.

It is important to remember here that the Christian community has a representative role, as sign and realisation of God's giving of himself to all men. All men are faced with the same basic structure of reality, the God-man relationship in Jesus Christ. Even when they do not explicitly understand this basis they can and do in their living activity and in their reflection, attain a great deal of insight into how men should behave and live in the actual situation in which they are. Not only then do we learn from the wider world much of the scientific knowledge relevant to our ethical understanding. We must also learn from their own ethical example and reflection. And they may well have in a particular area a more refined ethical understanding than that as yet attained by the Christian community. The resources available to the Christian community include those of the whole human community of which it is part, that part in which God's self-giving to man in Christ is explicitly recognised. The self-giving is in fact to the total community, and so the understanding depends on and should use the resources of the total community.

The community understanding will always be capable of further development because of man's historical condition. It may well be deficient even so far as this stage of development is concerned because of man's inherent weakness for which the Holy Spirit cannot always atone. As understanding of the Christian community it will then have varying degrees of authority and certainty. And it will have the necessary characteristic of all community understanding and formulation that it will be in general terms, outlining the basic structure of the Christian life or of a particular area in it. In so far as the basic structure is properly understood and expressed it will be verified in the particular person's individual situation, but how that basic structure is to take definite shape in a personal action may vary enormously. Here the creative capacity of the individual person must be taken into account as he responds to God and to neighbour within the community and using all the resources available to him from the community, yet in accordance with his own unique vocation, his own irreducible personality. To ignore or eliminate this uniqueness or irreducibility would be to destroy the community by turning it into an ant-heap. The personal understanding should integrate the community understanding in so far as that is truly expressive of the basic structure of reality in any area of moral activity. This could also be described by saying that such understandings or formulations express the elementary directions of moral activity. This is where some situationists make their mistake, ignoring or denying such a basic structure or at least its intelligibility. But not all community formulations express adequately this basic structure or elementary direction and even where they do, the personal action is much more than its basic structure or elementary direction and may be realised in innumerable forms and degrees. To ignore or deny this personal and creative aspect of moral activity has been the failure of the legal approach to morality.

3. THE CHRISTIAN ETHIC: FOR THE BUILDING OF A COMMUNITY

God spoke to man in community and his word can be properly understood only in community. The purpose and consequence of this speaking to man is the formation of a community. It is at this level that the community dimension of the Christian ethic most forcibly appears. The Word or self-giving of God to mankind forms mankind into a community. This is at once a gift and a task (*donum et mandatum*), something given and something yet to be achieved. The true response of man to God's gift is the promotion of the community of mankind, the development of mankind as God's people. Whatever human activity then promotes this community is a correct response to God, morally good activity; whatever activity hinders or disrupts the community is a failure in response, morally bad activity. Community building becomes the criterion or norm of morality. It is for this reason above all that one speaks of the Christian ethic as a community ethic.

To understand and establish this claim it is necessary to look again at the history of God's dealings with mankind in both the Old and New Testaments. The covenant on Sinai was a covenant with a people, but it was at the same time constitutive of a people. It was a climax to the events of the Exodus whereby God undertook the formation of the Israelites into a unified people with a distinct vocation in the world. It was his choice that made them a people, his people. By the acceptance of this covenant and the living of it they become not only united with him but also with one another. The moral demands of this covenant as enshrined in the Decalogue comprise obligations to Yahweh and to one another. These two are inseparable. So that if the Israelites will obey Yahweh's voice and keep his covenant they shall really become his people, 'a kingdom of priests and a holy nation' (*Ex.* 19:5f.).

Their failure to do this results in their punishment and dispersal from time to time. The post-Sinai history of Israel parallels the pre-Sinai history of mankind, with God's call to man being directed towards his development in unity or community by the use of the world's resources and with man's failure to respond to God resulting in division. The Adam and Eve story stresses their community both in origin and in love relationship, their distinction from the rest of the world and yet their harmonious lordship of it so long as they continued in the relationship of loving obedience with the Creator. The immediate consequence of their failure was division from each other, as shown in their covering of themselves and in Adam's blaming of the woman. The more profound human divisions caused by sin emerge in the following Cain and Abel story and in the events leading up to the Flood. The story of the Tower of Babel highlights the tragic division between men. In such close physical contiguity they were yet unable to speak to one another. The successive efforts of Yahweh through Noah and Abraham, through Moses and the prophets, are directed towards the formation of a people, a community through whom salvation would come to all mankind. The covenants, the other historical events, and the prophetic and wisdom literature are at once the product of a people (through God's self-giving) and also constitutive of that people. It is God's word to man that first of all establishes the human community at its true level. (Problems of monogenism and polygenism must be considered separately and are secondary to this basic truth.) The further growth of this community (a necessary dimension because of man's historical character) is distorted from the beginning by man's sin and is constantly threatened by sin. It is only the persistent loving of Yahweh that overcomes this distortion and makes the community of mankind continually possible.

When that persistent loving took concrete shape in the person of Jesus Christ a new stage in the realisation of the community of mankind was reached. Jesus' mission of redemption was the reconciliation of man with the Father and of man with man. The Father's love in sending his Son was the full expression of God's self-giving to man by becoming man, by entering into the human condition. The response which this demanded of man reached its fullness in the self-surrender of the man Jesus out of love for the Father and for mankind. By his life, death and resurrection Jesus Christ manifested God's way to man and man's way to God. The fruit of this was given to the world by the Pentecostal community and the miracle of tongues, which, neatly counter-pointing the divisions of Babel, shows the new communication possible between men.

This was achieved for man in community. The community was of course to be God's people, the new Israel. It was meant for all men, whether Jew or Gentile. But the basic source of its unity is manifest in Jesus Christ because all men are called to be united with him as sons (and daughters) of the Father and so brothers (and sisters) of one another. The unity of mankind is now seen not to rest on any biological, psychological, or sociological basis but on a theological one, in the literal sense of that term as pertaining to *Theou logos*, the Word of God. God's Word addressed to men is the basis of their unity. In the light of the New Testament revelation that Word is the personal being of the Second Person of the Trinity become man. In him and through him men exist, develop, and achieve their destiny, fullness of union with the Father and with one another.

It was because the true being of man was founded in this relationship of sonship and brotherhood that Jesus

E

could summarise the whole law and the prophets as love of God and love of neighbour. The primacy of charity in Christian teaching and living derives from this relational reality which men enjoy with the Father and with one another, a reality arising from the fact that God first loved us (1 *John* 4:10).

This is a single relational reality. Sonship of the Father equals brotherhood of Christ equals brotherhood of all men. There can be no question of separating them. It is impossible to love the Father without loving one another (1 *John* 4:20). While this reality and the recognition of it in love of God and of neighbour existed in the Old Testament (see *Deut.* 6:5; *Lev.* 19:18) it only appeared in its true dimension with the coming of the only-begotten Son of the Father. Because of the indivisibility of love of God and love of neighbour, Jesus would describe love of neighbour as the new commandment (*John* 13:34), the distinguishing sign of his followers (*John* 13:35), and the final criterion by which all men should be judged (*Matt.* 25:31ff.). Paul in his turn could reduce the whole law simply to love of neighbour (*Rom.* 13:8–10; *Gal.* 5:14). This is what the self-giving of God to the community demands, for God is love (1 *John* 4:16).

It is in the visible community of the Church that God's self-giving in Christ and his call to man to respond in this way breaks the surface, becomes perceptible in a human manner (*Lumen gentium,* ch. 1). The Church exists as a sign and realisation of God's community-forming love in the world (*ibid.*). It does not exist for its own sake but for the sake of mankind, to help form the true community of mankind or better to assist this community which in virtue of God's self-giving to mankind already exists to emerge more fully, to grow and develop (see *Gaudium et spes,* art. 77ff.).

The call to all men, then, is the call to the formation and development of the true human community. It is only in this community that the individual person reaches his own fulfilment. Wholly dependent at first on the resources of the community, as he matures he contributes to the community by his responsible human activity which is then judged to be good or bad as it is developing of the community or disruptive of it.

It is only in the Christian perspective that certain limitations inevitable in all efforts at building community can be understood.

Because man is a historical being, the human community is always building, always capable of further progress. A community ethic is necessarily a dynamic one. Because man enjoys a certain irreducible dignity as the term of divine and human love and as a source of love in his turn, the community cannot develop by the suppression or elimination or diminishment of the individual person. A Christian community ethic is necessarily a personal ethic. Because man has failed in love and so in his community relations, because he continually fails in some degree and is always threatened by total failure, the progress in community building is always ambiguous. A breakthrough in the technological or political unification of mankind does not necessarily bring an equal breakthrough in the growth of true human community. Yet it is with and through these technological, political, and other human means that men must work for the fuller and more genuine community of mankind.

Because in spite of man's failure the true community of mankind is based on the unfailing love of God manifested in Jesus Christ and proclaimed by his Church, the human community can never entirely break down and is assured of ultimate completion. But precisely because the complete unity of men with one another implies their complete unity with the Father, this complete unity lies beyond history, is eschatological. Then and only then will mankind share the fullness of sonship of the Father and of brotherhood with one another in the risen Christ.

It is for this final unity that the Church, that Christians, are working. But they have to work at it now. Their call is to enter fully into the task of developing the human community here on earth through the use of all resources, human and divine, available to them. In this way they promote the kingdom of God on earth, release men from the bonds of sin and selfishness, and humanise (Christianise) the cosmos by developing it in the service of mankind. In pursuit of this goal they seek to work with all men of goodwill in any project that will realise further the God-given unity of mankind. Because of their explicit awareness of the basis of this unity or community they will more urgently enter into the task of achieving it, and, while aware of the limitations of what may be humanly possible, never lose hope in the reconciling power of God's love.

The call of all men is to the building of the human community. All good human activity is community building activity. The true human ethic is a community ethic in this sense. For the Christian this call, finally manifest in Christ, comes from the Father, was given to man in community, can be understood only by man in community, and is directed towards the building of the true human community founded on man's sonship of the Father and brotherhood with all other men, both of which derive from and are manifest in Jesus Christ.

4

The Primacy of Charity

THAT charity enjoys a certain primacy in God's revelation of himself in the Old and New Testaments scarcely requires any demonstration for Christians. The two great commandments, as Christ calls them (*Matt.* 22:34–40; *Mark* 12:28–34; *Luke* 10:25–8), and which sum up for him the whole law and the prophets, were explicitly taken from the law, the law of the Old Testament or Mosaic covenant (*Deut.* 6:5; *Lev.* 19:18). In Christ's teaching they were expressly joined together, given a new extension and depth, but they had their place in the life of the old Israel as in that of the new. And the motif which dominates the relationship between God and the first people of his choice, is that of love, the love of a faithful husband for a frequently faithless wife (cf. *Hos.* 1–3).

This faithful love achieved the climax of its expression when the Father sent his only-begotten Son (*John* 3:16). And the understanding of this love and the range of its application underwent such a development that Christ could speak of it as his new commandment (*John* 13:34) and the distinguishing feature of his followers for the whole world (*John* 13:35). In his person, life and teaching, Christ reveals the scope and demands of charity in the life and behaviour of his followers. And the theological reflection recorded in John's first epistle underlines the implications of the new commandment as he insists on love of neighbour as the ultimate criterion of love of God (1 *John* 3:17; 4:20–21). For Paul the more excellent way of charity gives meaning to everything else that a man does (1 *Cor.* 12:31; 13:1ff.). It is the bond of perfection (*Col.* 3:14) in which all the other moral precepts are fulfilled (*Rom.* 13:8–10; *Gal.* 5:14).

In attempting a scientific account of the behaviour demanded of Christ's followers, moral theology must in its general and special sections accord to charity the recognition given to it by Christ and the inspired writers. Our purpose here is to explore what this recognition means and why it may be described as the primacy of charity in moral theology. The pursuit of this purpose must be within the general framework of the God-Christ-man relationship and of the invitation-response structure which underlies the Christian life and moral theology.

A Divine Gift

There is of course nothing that we have not received from God (1 *Cor.* 4:7). The whole of creation is a reflection of God, some communication, however inadequate, of the divine goodness. Man created in the image of God (*Gen.* 1:26), enjoying at the human-created level capacities to know and love, so characteristic of God himself, must be regarded as the omega-point of God's gift of creation. Yet to talk of charity or Christian love as a divine gift is to transcend the created and human for the divine itself, to move from reflection and image to that which is reflected and imaged. Charity is God abroad in the world (1 *John* 4:16–17). It is a divine gift, a gift by the divine of the divine.

The two primary commandments for man are his love of God and his love of his neighbour for God's sake. But they are secondary to and derivative from God's love of him. The agape-love of the New Testament to which man is summoned springs from God's love of man. 'In this is love, not that we loved God, but that he loved us' (1 *John* 4:10). God's approach to man in love in the Old and New Testaments, which is recounted in the history of salvation, has a transforming effect on man. This presence of God to man in love enables man to love in return. 'See what love the Father has given us that we should be called the children of God; and so we are' (1 *John* 3:1; cf. *Rom.* 8:16; 1 *John* 3:10).

Love awakens love. The love of the Father for man awakens in him a new capacity to love. Man receives not only a new grasp of God's lovableness, so that he may be stimulated to a greater intensity of love. He is caught up by the power of God's love into loving as God does. God's communication of love is a communication of the power to love as Christ loves, as God loves (cf. *John* 15:9–12). So man becomes in a superhuman way like to God, sharing the divine love, participating in the internal divine life. In his offer of love God offers and communicates himself, for God is love. In responding to this communication man loves with the love of God. The charity which unites him to God and his fellowman comes entirely from God. For it is 'God's love (which) has been poured into our hearts through the Holy Spirit which has been given to us' (*Rom.* 5:5).

The Personal Quality of Charity

The divine gift which is charity presupposes a certain capacity in man. It is only because man is a loving creature that he can be admitted to sharing the love of the Creator. The spiritual dimension which distinguishes man from the most highly developed animal or the most intricate machine and which constitutes him a person, enables him to love. Love is a relationship between two persons. It is in fact *the* relationship between them. Only persons can love and be loved.

A love relationship is easier to recognise in the concrete than to analyse it in the abstract. Witnessing the love of a mother for her child, of friend for friend, of husband for wife can be far more enlightening than any abstract discussion. Yet to understand the gift of charity, it is necessary to examine more fully the nature and characteristics of love at this human and personal level.

Love may be generally described as a profound personal recognition of and inclination towards another person seeking unity with him. This movement arises from the depth of one's personality where mind and will and feeling merge. Love offers self to the other in search of unity. Where the love is mutual, unity is achieved; a community is formed.

The personal reaction of love for another begins with some recognition, however implicit and inarticulate, of the loved one as valuable in himself, an end in himself and not just a means. This value derives from his unique, irreplaceable character and the autonomy which he enjoys as a spiritual being.

Part of creation and so reflecting the divine, part of the human race and so an image of God, each human being enjoys personal uniqueness before God and so before other men. He reflects and images God in a way impossible to anything or anybody else. He is the incarnation of a human spirit with an unrepeated name and destiny, an irreproducible capacity to love. Genuine love requires this uniqueness. It does not love mankind. It loves men, particular people, whom it recognises in this personal way. A mother loves her children not in general but each of them in a special individual way.

Closely related to this unique quality of the person is his autonomy. Through his spiritual endowment he possesses the power of self-determination, the right to dispose of self, to commit himself. He and no other human being is master of his destiny. This is the meaning of his free will. (In both his uniqueness and his autonomy, he is manifesting in the highest earthly form the one, omnipotent God.) The personal reaction of love recognises this autonomy. It never seeks to possess or use a person as one might possess or use a thing. The possessive mother or lover is so far deficient in love. The loved one may not be sought for self-satisfaction, used just to fulfil one's needs. Such a movement would imprison the beloved (and indeed the lover) and destroy his autonomy. His integrity as a person is violated. Instead of being accepted as a person (a thou or you, in the Buber terminology), he becomes a thing (an it).[1]

The opening out to or movement towards the other in this way which is the beginning of love, demands further expression in care and service.[2] The care and service take different forms in different relationships. Not all loving care can be manifested in the same tender way as a mother's care for her new-born child. Not all mothers with a genuine love of their children will have the same manner or degree of tender care. But without care and service, love remains notional and unreal, a love of self perhaps or a love of the idea of love. The service also implies taking some responsibility for the beloved. His good becomes the personal concern of the lover, who will make his own the task of fostering that good and removing the dangers that threaten it.

Love draws the person out of himself towards the other in recognising and caring for the other and seeking unity with him. This movement outwards enables the person who loves to grow and develop. Without it he remains confined within himself, unable to expand as a person. In this sense a person needs to love. And since love is something which is gradually developed, and since it is essentially a response to another person, it flourishes only where there is a return of love. A person also needs to be loved. It is through loving that the person expresses himself most fully, that he attains his highest fulfilment as a person. It is by being loved that his own love and capacity to love are completed and reassured. Love is the necessary perfection of the person and it is love which stimulates or creates love.

Here some brief reference to the age-old discussion between the giving and the receiving aspects of love is necessary. Does somebody love for what he gets or for what he gives? Is love a form of desire, a search for something for oneself, some pleasure or satisfaction, or is it disinterested giving to another? The discussion has been carried on in the context of merely human love and of Christian charity. St Thomas distinguished between a love of desire, *amor con-cupiscentiae,* which sought primarily the good of the lover, and love of benevolence, *amor benevolentiae,* which sought primarily the good of the beloved.[3] The distinction was described by C. S. Lewis as that of 'need love' and 'gift love'[4] and a similar distinction is basic to Nygren's important work, *Agape and Eros.*[5]

Because man needs to love and to be loved, it might seem that his love is necessarily a 'need love' or selfish love. But this is to misunderstand the personality of man and his need to love. In his human endowment man has been given the capacity to recognise and love the other for the other's sake, as a unique autonomous person, valuable in himself. In doing this the lover is both giving and receiving. But he receives only to the extent that he gives. The disinterested self-giving is primary, but can be achieved in various degrees and only gradually. If, however, he seeks only his own satisfaction, he does not love in authentic fashion and he fails to break out of his self-enclosure and reach the other as another person.[6] He remains confined within this self-centred circle and is unable to expand and develop. His attempt to love only for his own sake destroys love and prevents his normal personal fulfilment.

The divine love which man shares in charity, respects his human condition and operates through it. But a new superhuman dimension has been introduced. In the loving relationship with the personal God which he enjoys, the recognition and service and self-giving are not from his own resources. He has been admitted to the personal life and love of the Trinity, so that he loves in some measure as God loves. His love of human persons has been transformed in this way also, so that he sees and loves them as God sees and loves them. His recognition and service and love still depend on his human faculties and human activities; but they have been deepened by faith, so that he recognises more deeply the value and lovableness (the divine lovableness) of each person, and seeks unity with them under the impelling force of God's love for them.

At this divine level also the apparent conflict between 'need love' and 'gift love' is more clearly transcended.[7] The total giving of the divine persons to each other without losing their identity as persons provides the supreme model of 'gift love'. It is on this model and through enjoying some share in the actual trinitarian love and giving, that man gives himself in charity to God and his fellowmen.

Christian Love

Charity is God's love abroad in the world. It is the presence of God in love to the human person, asking for love in response. It is the presence of God in love within the human person, seeking expression through his human and personal activity. It was in Christ that this loving presence of God to man and man's loving response achieved supreme realisation. It is by each man's union with Christ that the divine love enters his heart and elicits his response. Christ is the love-link between God and man; God's communication of himself as love to man. In the person and life of Christ charity entered fully into man's world.

It was out of love for the world, for man, in the desire to share his divine, eternal life with him, that God sent his only Son (*John* 3:36). This initiative born of love was all the more striking in that it was while we were yet sinners (*Rom.* 5:8; cf. *Eph.* 2:4–5) that 'God sent his only son into the world so that we might live through him' (1 *John* 4:9). The plan of salvation for man which the Father accomplished in Christ, was at once a manifestation of the divine love and an invitation to love. It manifested the divine love by manifesting the God who is love. Christ reveals the Father. He who sees him, sees the Father (*John* 14:9). He who hates him, hates the Father (*John* 15:23). No one can come in love to the Father except through him (*John* 14:6). If a man loves him, Christ and the Father will love him and they will come and dwell with him (*John* 14:23). He himself manifested the highest love for the Father (*John* 14:31) and for man by laying down his life for man (*John* 15:13) to atone for man's previous rejection of God and restore him to the Father. And in his return to the Father he sent as he had promised the Spirit (*John* 14:16), the mutual love-gift of Father and Son. The reception of this Spirit, variously called the 'Spirit of God' (*Rom.* 8:9, 14; *Eph.* 4:30), the 'Spirit of Christ' (*Rom.* 8:9), the 'Spirit of the Son' (*Gal.* 4:6), completed the admission of his friends to the divine life, giving them the rank of sons of the Father and brothers of Christ (*Rom.* 8:15; *Eph.* 4:6–7).

In his personal life and teaching Christ gave his followers the example and instruction by which they were to fulfil the two great commandments. Through his death and resurrection he assured them of the power to follow this example and instruction. By abiding in the vine and sharing its life Christians bear fruit (*John* 15:1ff.) in the recognition and service and union of love with God and man. By being united with their head in one body (1 *Cor.* 12:12–27; *Eph.* 4:1–16) they experience the impulse of the love that was in Christ. In this way they are able to fulfil his new commandment (*John* 13:34) to love as he loves, as sons of the Father and brothers of Christ.

This divine love was always active in the world, even after man's sin. The whole history of salvation testifies to the persistence of the Father in seeking man's love. The promise of a redeemer after man's initial failure, the slow patient fulfilment of that promise in the call of Abraham, the definitive call of the people of Israel in the Exodus and in the giving of the Mosaic law, the sending of the prophets— these provided continual reminders and manifestations of God's love. In his instructions and commandments also the God of Israel, the God of the Old Testament, revealed the importance of love. Yet it was with the sending of his Son that his love and he himself as love were fully manifested to man and the power to share that love made freely available to him.

A Crucified Love

Christian love is born in the shadow of the cross, where Christ for love of man finally and totally surrendered himself in love to the Father. It was for this that he came into the world, to do the will of him who sent him 'so that the world might know that I love the Father' (*John* 14:31). The fulfilment of the Father's will to save mankind involved placing a certain distance between himself and the Father. He came out from the Father to share man's lowly and unglorified condition. Although he was the only-begotten Son he emptied himself, taking the form of a servant, like to man in all things except sin (*Phil.* 2:6–7). He was to return to the Father and share again the glory which was his from the beginning (*John* 17:5, 24). But his very return was the way of fallen mankind, the way of disintegration and death. In accepting humanity he also accepted death. The particularly painful and brutal death which Christ experienced impresses on us the extent of his love. But the primary fact is that he died. God-made-man died. He went to his Father through the way imposed on man for his sin (*Rom.* 5:12), and he experienced all the fear and agony which are man's facing the wrenching apart of body and spirit. He shrank from it, as men do. He begged the Father to save him from it, if possible (*Matt.* 26:39). He cried out in abandonment during the last moments (*Matt.* 27:46). Christ was not playing at being a man. He was fully human and paid the price of his humanity in leaving this world.

Some other way of reconciling man with God could have been devised. But the effectiveness of the way chosen may at least be partially grasped. In the undeniable reality of Christ's human life taken to its bitter end, in the personal acceptance of this death despite the human revulsion from it, the meaning of the divine love for mankind, of the love expected in return from man in the context of sin and its consequences, could hardly be made clearer. It is in contemplating the climax of Christ's life in his death, that one begins to appreciate 'the breadth and length and height and depth' of his love, a love 'that surpasses knowledge', and by which 'we are filled with the fullness of God' (*Eph.* 3:18–19).

It was necessary in the Father's plan for Christ to pass through the separation of death to enter into the glory of the resurrection (*Luke* 24:26). The reconciliation and reunion of God and man at Christ's glorification in the resurrection were achieved for sinful mankind through Christ's sacrifice of himself on the cross (*Rom.* 5:10–11; *Eph.* 2:13–16). Whoever would follow Christ in his loving surrender to the Father, must understand that the way of Christian love, as marked out by Christ, is the way of the cross (*Matt.* 16:24).

Christians are baptised into the passion, death and resurrection of Christ (*Rom.* 6:3ff.). Their Christian life is a living out of these redemptive mysteries in their own life. Their identification with Christ in his total giving of himself to the Father is realised first of all in the sacramental meeting with Christ. Each sacrament provides its particular contact with Christ in the mystery of his self-giving and the Father's acceptance through death and resurrection. The basic sacramental introduction to Christ in his redemptive activity takes place at baptism, gateway to the Church and to the other sacraments. Its climax is reached in the Eucharist which makes present not merely Christ in action, acting on the recipient, but Christ in person, and unites man directly to the redemptive sacrifice of the cross and its glorious completion.

Christian love then is stamped with the sign of the cross. The sacramental way of union with Christ emphasises this. But behind the cross lies man's sin. In the divine plan, Christ's death was the result of man's sin (*Rom.* 5:6 ff. etc.) Man by his rejection of God had lost contact with the focal point of his existence and of his love. His capacity and need to love were frustrated. His love, cut off from its ultimate, meaningful term in the person of God, turned in on himself. He became imprisoned in the self, unable of himself to reach even other human persons in complete love-relationships. It was in this failure to love others with the disinterested recognition and service which such love implies, that man's sin made itself most evident in his human activity. His essential humanity remained, but because his personal link with God had been broken, his other personal links lacked vitality. To break out of the circle of self became increasingly difficult, and other people tended to become objects of satisfaction, things to be used rather than people to be loved.

The breakthrough from self to the Father and to other men was achieved supremely for sinful man by Christ. In the climax of his self-giving, in his passion and death, Christ taught man how he must die to self to reach the other and so love in a fully personal way. Breaking out of his shell of selfishness in which he has become fixed through sin and its consequences, is a very painful process for man. The pain is completed by death to the old self-centred sinful man (*Rom.* 6:5–6), who is crucified (*Gal.* 5:24). Thereby man rises with Christ to a new life (*Rom.* 6:4; *Col.* 2:12ff. etc.). He is a new man (*Eph.* 2:15), a new creation (2 *Cor.* 5:17).[8] The share in Christ's death and resurrection which is man's through the sacraments must be translated into his everyday activity. The pain and death will be no longer simply his in sign and in the presence of Christ with him, but in the experience of trying to give himself after the manner of Christ to God and his neighbour. Every attempt to do this will involve suffering, the suffering of placing others before oneself, of letting go of oneself to reach the others. Gradually man through the power of Christ's love will acquire mastery over himself. He will become in spirit and action another son of God, liberated from the slavery of sin and of self. But the process will be slow and painful, making continuous demands upon him in his every human act and contact. Each day he has to die to self, overcoming his selfish tendencies, giving himself out of love to the recognition and service of God and mankind. But it is by dying with Christ in this way that he experiences the joy of Christ's resurrection, losing his life to find it anew in the joy (*John* 16:20–24; *Rom.* 14:17; 15:13) and peace (*John* 14:27; *Rom.* 14:17; 15:13) and liberty (*Rom.* 8:21; 2 *Cor.* 3:17) of the sons of God.

Love of God and of Man

The object of charity, its personal term, is both God and man. This was already laid down in the Mosaic law, although the immediate linking of the two commandments and their recognition as summarising the whole law was only made explicit in the new law. The further implications of the New Testament relation between those commandments gradually emerge in the teaching of Jesus and his apostles.

Love of man, love of neighbour, assumes a new significance as the test of one's love of God. No man can claim to love God unless he has a genuine love of his neighbour (1 *John* 4:20). Jesus' description of his second coming and man's final judgement (*Matt.* 25:31–46) makes this very clear. Our living recognition and service of Christ depends on recognition and service of him in the poor and needy who inhabit our world. To fail these people is to fail Christ. To ignore their poverty, illness, and other needs is to ignore Christ.

The image of God in the neighbour, which is the source of his personality, his uniqueness and his lovableness, has received a new depth through the incarnation. All men are now called to be sons of the Father. They must be loved and served as Christ must be loved and served, as they share his sonship and lovableness. This applies to all mankind. There can be no distinction of race or class or creed. One must love all as Christ loves them, even one's enemies (*Matt.* 5:43–8), so that the Christian return for hate, persecution and death is love. 'Father forgive them . . . ' (*Luke* 23:34).

The love of neighbour required of Christians is clearly an active love. The emphasis in Jesus' account of the final judgement, as in his parable of the good Samaritan (*Luke* 10:29–37), is on the need to express love in service of the poor and needy. The sins of omission loom much larger here than they were allowed to in the conventional Christian exhortation. To ignore and neglect the hungry, the sick, the home-less, the under-privileged of any kind, merits Christ's 'Depart from me'. Matthew 25 should make disturbing reading for the comfortable Western Christian, lay or cleric, who preserves his peace of mind by playing down the victimisa-tion that is all about him, or who invokes a misguided prudence in support of the status quo and inactivity, even if it is called 'gradualness'. The vitality of Christianity (for example, of Christian love) in any society and in the whole world is measured not by external religious trappings, but by the dynamic efforts of the strong (strong politically, fin-ancially or educationally) to help, in the name of Christ, the weak.

Christian love demands service but it must be personal service, as the love is personal. Charity does not mean primarily dispensing alms or providing social service. It is first of all recognising, respecting and committing oneself to a person. It may happen in a fleeting encounter, yet the respect and reverence and love for the other will be sufficient to manifest the community which exists between all men in Christ. Just as it is possible to degrade a person by using him as an object or possession, so it is possible to give help in an impersonal and degrading way. Without genuine concern and love for the person in need, the assistance becomes a form of self-satisfaction for the individual or society. Love and service go together. And true love demands efficient service, the organised assistance of the weak in today's complex world. But such assistance must always recognise the first need of these people, to be treated and respected and loved as people.

Love is a relation between persons. It involves the whole person, his mind in recognising the other person, his will in self-commitment to him, his emotions in support of both. Where mind and will and feeling harmonise, love flourishes. But if the recognition of the other as a person, and as this particular person, is weak or underdeveloped, or if the will to commitment is hampered by self-will, or if there is some

F

emotional reaction against the other, love is weak and may perish.

The pulpit cliché, 'You must love but need not like', can be very misleading here. The accompanying explanation that love is an act of the will not of the emotions, and that you cannot control or at least command your likes and dislikes, is inadequate. The act of choice by the will is the finally decisive element in love. And one can love even where there is emotional revulsion. But this is an abnormal situation. Love is an activity of the whole person and the will is heavily conditioned by the mental and emotional reaction of the person. Unless an attempt is made to resolve the emotional dislike, the love will not survive for long, as the person's thought, speech and activity may quickly demonstrate. Christian loving should normally involve liking, or at least gradually remove any disliking of persons.[9]

Charity and the Other Virtues

The supremacy of charity in the Christian life and amongst the virtues is incontestable as far as the evidence of revelation goes. In the theological understanding of this, there have been various stages of development. A climax was reached in medieval theology with St Thomas. His description[10] of charity as mother, basis and root of all the virtues received its full doctrinal expression in his teaching on charity as the form of the virtues.[11] Today, after many changes of direction and some very mistaken attempts to give charity its due place, a fresh attempt is being made to probe the relationship between charity and the other virtues in the Christian ethic.

The primacy of Christian charity over the other virtues derives from the place of love as man's supreme personal activity, and the essentially divine character of Christian love as a share in the divine love. Through it man loves with the love of God himself. But this love must be active, express itself in reverence and service of God and man. The explicit teaching of the New Testament as well as the peculiar nature

of man as a material spiritual being who expresses himself
and develops through his human activity, make it clear that
charity requires the various activities of the other virtues,
truth, chastity and the rest. That charity must be active is, as
was pointed out above, an absolutely basic Christian require-
ment. So any form of quietism, which would suppress all
other human activity in favour of pure acts of charity,
cannot be reconciled with Christ's own teaching and has
been very properly condemned by the Church.[12]

A different and more subtle misunderstanding of the
primacy of charity has been given new vitality in recent
times. It accepts the other virtues of justice, chastity etc., and
some formulations of their content and limits in commands
and prohibitions, as general guide-lines for the Christian.
But it maintains that these formulations of limits in the
prohibition of fornication, for example, can never be absolute.
What is ultimately decisive in an ethical situation, is how far
the activity contemplated is an expression of love. And one
can never *a priori* rule out any particular activity, such as
fornication, as always and ever incompatible with true
Christian love and, therefore, as absolutely forbidden. In
ninety-nine cases out of a hundred perhaps it will be so,
but there is the possibility of the hundredth case.[13]

This approach, a form of 'situation ethics' rife in Europe
in the forties and fifties, has come very much to the fore
amongst English-speaking Christians in the sixties, through
the take over writings of John A. T. Robinson,[14] Canon
Douglas Rhymes[15] and others. There should be no denying
the merit of their approach in emphasising again the central
role of chairty for too long neglected in the conventional
Catholic moral teaching at least. The preoccupation for so
long with the physical integrity of sexual acts, for example,
together with the neglect of the more fundamental problem of
whether this act was a genuine expression of Christian love,
provides a classic instance of the type of Christian moral
teaching against which the then bishop and the canon were
reacting. Yet their ethic, despite its apparent support from

Augustine's summary of Christian living, *ama et fac quod vis*, empties love of any real meaning, ignores man's human condition and is ultimately opposed to the teaching of the New Testament.

To maintain that while love generally expresses itself in a particular way and generally excludes certain actions, there are no actions which could not in certain circumstances be compatible with it, does seem, as Herbert McCabe points out, to make love meaningless.[16] If, for example, 'rape' or 'cruelty to children', carefully defined of course, could be regarded as expressions of love in some conceivable circumstances, love loses all meaning. If they could not, then there are some absolutes in the Christian ethic, some activities absolutely forbidden, some limits to the behaviour which can be an expression of love. Genuine Christian love then demands avoidance of such behaviour. Virtues and vices, commands and prohibitions, retain their reality under the primacy of love.

The deeper basis for this lies in man's human condition. Created in God's image with a capacity to know, to commit himself freely, to love, called to a divine destiny to share in the divine knowledge and love, man is a complex material-spiritual creature. He is a social being, destined to enter the world and develop in it through relationships with others. He is a sexual being. He is a being in time, who develops gradually. Within this divinely given structure man seeks his destiny, seeks to express, through the human faculties or powers with which he has been endowed, the divine love given to him. The expression of this love from God is possible only through the human faculties also received from God. So it is possible to see that not every conceivable act respects this divinely given structure and so some such actions could not be ways of communicating charity. What precisely these forbidden actions are or how far they extend may be difficult to determine, although there is a long history of human reflection on this problem with some fairly widespread agreement on matters like murder, lying, adultery.

However, it is in the New Testament that any doubts about whether love suppresses in this 'situation' sense the need for the other virtues, are removed. Jesus is very insistent that whoever loves must keep his commandments (*John* 14:15), and these are often a reaffirmation, extension and deepening of the commandments received by Moses from Yahweh (cf. *Matt.* 5:17–48). They clearly include the prohibition of those actions which could not possibly be bearers or expressions of Christian love because they defile man,[17] and which are listed by St Paul as evil and excluding from the kingdom of heaven (*Rom.* 1:28–31; *Gal.* 5:19–21). The explicit teaching of the New Testament and its authentication for succeeding generations by Christ's Church, demonstrate the possible and impossible ways of communicating Christian charity. In their positive content and negative limits, the other virtues have an irreplaceable role in Christian life as a life of love.

The primary role of love in the Christian life as giving all other virtues their true Christian or divine significance[18] has been expressed in St Thomas' doctrine of charity as the *forma omnium virtutum*. The moral goodness of a particular human activity or virtue is derived from its relation to man's last end.[19] It is this relation which basically gives the act or virtue its form.[20] But this relation is the relation of charity uniting the human agent with God as his last end. So charity constitutes the 'form' of all the virtues, as well as being the mother which nourishes them, the foundation on which they are laid, the root from which they grow.[21]

One understanding of St Thomas' teaching regards this relation to the last end given to a virtuous act by charity as extrinsic to the act itself. A man performs these acts out of charity, for love of God. Acts of justice and of the other virtues are referred to God from the outside by the human agent. Charity does not enter into the object of the act in an intrinsic way.

The recent work of Gerard Gillemann[22] has challenged this both as an adequate explanation of the relationship between charity and the other virtues and as a correct understanding of St Thomas. For him the relationship is intrinsic, in the very act itself, so that this action of justice, for example, is a mediation of charity in this sphere of life. The acts of the other virtues are mediations or communications of charity in different areas of life. In this line of argument the object of any particular virtue is a particular *finis, bonum* or value which derives its meaning and existence from the supreme value, the *summum bonum* or *finis ultimus*, God. The fundamental relationship of the person to God which is charity, is mediated or participated in by the particular virtue or activity which relates the person to this particular good of, for example, justice or chastity.

In revealing the internal dynamism of charity as it seeks expression through man's human endowment in the various virtuous activities, Gillemann has done a great service to moral theology. And he has shown fairly convincingly that the divine love is not merely a source of inspiration or motivation, but the very motor-force[23] or efficient cause[24] which finds expression in all the Christian's good acts; so that these acts are in the abstract to be regarded as good if they are capable of being expressions of the divine love in man. Man's complex make-up, and the complexity of particular goods or values through which he is perfected, demand different forms of such expression, just as they rule out others.

Difficulties about the distinction of the other virtues from charity, and the meaning of 'virtuous' activity in somebody without charity, are not insuperable. To the plurality of particular virtues or ends open to man in his complexity, must be added his temporal character, his living in time. It is only gradually, one step after another, that man, entering into himself, taking possession of himself, achieves these particular values. He can achieve any or all of these in some degree without attaining the supreme virtue of his being, his giving of himself as a whole in love. But the realisation of these particular values by acts of justice or truth or chastity is directed towards and needs to be completed in love. It is as expressions of love that they are fully acts of any particular virtue. These points are further developed in an article by Karl Rahner,[25] who goes on to stress an important distinction between charity and the other virtues.[26] While the other virtues demand certain actions from a man, charity demands himself. The other virtues gradually grow through exercise, but may be satisfied here and now through a particular action. Charity must be always growing and can never rest satisfied with the status quo. He who decides that he has given all in love, and that he cannot and will not love any more, has not really given all and does not love, as Christ commands, 'with all his heart and all his soul, with all his mind and all his strength' (*Mark* 12:30–31; cf. *Matt.* 22:37; *Luke* 10:27).

Conclusion

To recognise the primacy of charity in Christian life and in moral theology is to follow the spirit and the letter of the New Testament. The fuller understanding of charity as the Father's gift of the divine love, given to each man in Christ by the sending of the Spirit, and involving man in the pain and joy of Christ's death and resurrection, reveals the Christian's source of life and strength. It indicates what is precisely divine and Christian about him, his admission to the divine family as a son of the Father and brother of Christ. This divine and Christian element in him seeks expression through all his human powers and activities. It gives them their eternal relevance, as elements in the process of his christification, his gradual attainment of the fullness of life which the Son shares with the Father and the Holy Spirit.

The Father has invited all men to share this life in his Son. The mission of the Son, sent out of love, dedicating himself in love to the service of mankind, finally sacrificing himself in love to the Father for man—this mission continues to the end. But the Son is no longer physically present, no longer visible to man whom he would have to share his life.

It is in the members of his body, united with him and with each other, that the sacrificial love of Christ for mankind is now made visible. This is the sign of his disciples. It is this love, Christ's own love in his members, that must mediate the divine presence to men and evoke their love in return. The mission of the Church, of Christians, is to awaken men to the sense of God's presence among them by the force of Christian charity. For charity is God's presence in the world. Therein lies its primacy.

5

Penance and Charity

CHRISTIANITY offers and demands a way of life that is a way of love. So it was summarised as love of God and love of neighbour by its founder, Jesus Christ. The rediscovery by moral theology of the centrality of charity is one of the consoling advances of our time. That it should *need* to be rediscovered in the systematic theology of Christian behaviour is somewhat less consoling. However, it seems unlikely that this central role of charity, source and form of all other Christian virtues, will be obscured very quickly again. Perhaps the new danger to it may be from a verbal emphasis which cheapens it, emptying it of its true human and divine content. To avoid that it is necessary to set charity in its correct biblical and Christian context. Penance forms an essential part of that context.

If Jesus summarised his message as one of charity, it was not in these terms that he introduced it. His first preaching as recorded in the synoptic gospels and St John is a clarion call of another kind, a call to penance. 'Now after John was arrested, Jesus came into Galilee, preaching the gospel of God, and saying, "The time is fulfilled, and the kingdom of God is at hand; repent, and believe in the gospel"' (*Mark* 1:14f. cf. *Matt.* 4:12–17 and *Luke* 4:14–15). In introducing his message and himself in this way Jesus was following his immediate herald and predecessor John. A few verses earlier in Mark's gospel we read: 'John the baptiser appeared in the wilderness, preaching a baptism of repentance for the forgiveness of sins' (*Mark* 1:4). The parallel in Matthew (3:1–2) reads: 'In those days came John the Baptist, preaching in the wilderness of Judea, "Repent, for the kingdom of heaven is at hand"' (cf. *Luke* 3:2f.).

John himself was the last and the greatest of the prophets sent by Yahweh to his people Israel. The message of the prophets had been one of repentance for an Israel straying after false gods, a message of return to its one true God, Yahweh (cf. *Is.* 1:2ff.; *Jer.* 25:5–6; *Ezek.* 14:6; 18:30, 32; *Hos.* 12:6; *Joel* 2:12), of the faithless wife Israel to the faithful husband Yahweh (*Jer.* 3:2; *Hos.* 1–3), of rebellious subjects to their rightful king (cf. *Jer.* 3:12f.). The prophetic message of repentance reissued by the Father in Jesus Christ with a finality hitherto impossible, inevitably formed the introduction to the preaching of the men Jesus commissioned to bring his gospel to the ends of the earth. In answer to the question of those who gathered to hear the first Pentecost preaching, 'Brethren, what shall we do?' Peter replied, 'Repent and be baptised every one of you in the name of Jesus Christ for the forgiveness of your sins, and you shall receive the gift of the Holy Spirit . . . '(*Acts* 2:37ff.). The pattern is confirmed right through the first apostolic and Pauline preaching (cf. *Acts* 3:19; 5:31; 8:22; 11:18; 17:30; 20:21; 26:20).

For an adequate understanding of the Christian message the relation between charity as the heart of the message and penance as its introduction must be explored. In the light of the biblical usage, the English word 'repentance' (to a lesser extent 'conversion') seems more helpful in describing the reality involved and will be freely used.

Sin and Repentance in Salvation History

The central reality described and realised in the event of Christianity is the relationship between God and man. On his own initiative God entered man's world and set up a personal relationship between himself and man. He revealed or communicated himself by giving himself out of love to man and asking for man's love in return.

Like the human love-relationships that we know, the God-man relationship has a history. And this history is at once tragic and glorious. Tragic because it is the story of man's persistent failure to return love for love, of his continued disruption of the relationship, of his sin. Glorious because of God's persistent loving in spite of that sin and because of the eventual triumph of that love in the sending of his Son. In the person, life, death and resurrection of Jesus Christ the divine self-giving in love and the human response of love reached their completion. In its new head Jesus Christ, mankind responded to God in the manner appropriate, as at once truly man and Son of the Father.

The divine revelation or self-giving was then an invitation to man to love God in return. But from the beginning, because of man's sinfulness, it became an invitation to repent, to return to the relationship with the true God which man had disrupted. Repentance or return, conversion, penance, these are different words for the same reality, and a predominant theme in the history of the divine invitation as a result of man's sin.

In entrusting himself to man, God had to take man as he found him. This meant, for instance, that he had to approach man as a knowing, free being. Without the human capacity to know, to choose freely or to commit oneself there would be no question of a divine invitation to man, or of a God-man personal relationship. This ability to know and to respond freely involves the risk of man's refusal, of sin, but also in the context of his full humanity, the capacity to repent of that refusal, to return again to God.

That full humanity includes the community and historical dimensions of man. God had to and did approach man in community and in history. This emerges in its full explicitness in the history of the community or people of Israel. He chose this people as his people. He gave himself to them as their God. And this relationship was worked out in a history that centred about the formation of the people as a people in the Exodus and Mosaic covenant. But these events were the completion of one historical phase and the start of another. This people was chosen from all the peoples of the earth to be Yahweh's people as the sign and realisation of his call to all men. It was only when this people reached its definitive historical climax in Jesus Christ that its true character was revealed. Then it was transformed into the new Israel which incorporated God's explicit call to all men, whether Jew or Greek, bond or free.

The knowing, free, community and historical dimensions of man belonged to him as he came from God. In taking man as he found him in these ways, God was taking him as he created him. And they form the source and conditions of what is called repentance. But the necessity of repentance arose from man's first and repeated rejection of God's advances. It is demanded because of the way man turned out, not because of the way God turned him out. It is demanded because of sin. So the history of the God-man relationship became the history of repeated divine attempts to overcome human failure by greater love and to save man from the consequences of his failure. It became the history of salvation. Salvation, redemption, repentance are all characteristic and essential Christian words. They describe the effect or quality of divine love in face of human sin.

Repentance or Return through Jesus Christ

The depth of this refusal of sin, the lengths to which God was prepared to go to overcome it and the pain which man's return from sin involved, were fully revealed by God's sending of his Son and by the death on the cross through which man's definitive return to the Father was achieved.

Jesus had to take this way of return because of man's sin. The fullness of his response was expressed in his laying down of his life freely (*John* 10:18). Sinless himself in going out from the Father he accepted the full demands of the human condition (*Phil.* 2:5–8). Like to men in everything but sin (*Heb.* 4:15) his response to the Father and to men had to be in a sinful human context in which the rejection of God was more immediately expressed in the rejection of man (*Matt.* 25) and the two rejections were completely identified in the rejection of the God-man by his own people (*John* 1:11) who were God's people.

The passion and death of Christ express the penitential return aspect of man's response to God, as the resurrection expresses its triumphant completion. The direct applicability of this to all appears in the terms of Jesus' invitation to his disciples. The radical character of this call which gradually emerges in the gospel story is summed up in the demand to follow Jesus by taking up one's cross and by losing one's life as he did in order to find it (*Matt.* 16:24ff.).

The apostolic teaching of repentance (cf. *Acts* 4:9–12) became in concrete terms the preaching of Christ crucified (and so glorified). The shocking or scandalous character of this preaching, in Paul's description (1 *Cor.* 1:23), should not be obscured by any comforting explanations. It is in fact shocking because it defies easy explanation and yet challenges our intelligence to grapple with a more than human truth, the truth of man's rejection of God's love, and the way of painful, indeed mortal, return.

Death as the wages of sin (*Rom.* 6:23) has been conquered by the dying of Jesus. It has been transformed by his full and free entry into the whole painful disintegrating process, to make it a true passover from the threshold relationship with God possible in this earthly existence to the fullness of union attainable only in the heavenly existence. And the pain and disintegration of it from a personal and not merely biological point of view, the fear and sense of abandonment which Jesus also experienced (*Matt.* 26:36–45; 27:46), are the results of sin and have been made the means of our sanctification, the way of our return with Jesus to the Father.

The Threat of False Gods

In understanding the scandal of Jesus' death, and so the Christian meaning of penance, it is helpful to consider the biblical notion of sin as the pursuit of false gods in place of the one true God, Yahweh. The Mosaic covenant, whereby Yahweh was established as God of the people of Israel and the people of Israel established as his people, was at the same time a task. The way of life of the people had to incorporate and express this essential demand of him who was the Lord their God, that they should have no other gods before him. He was a jealous God who would not tolerate the bowing down before or serving of idols (*Exod.* 20:1–4). The further history of the covenant reveals Israel's future in this task of truly knowing Yahweh. The prophetic call to repentance during that history was a call to a genuine recognition of Yahweh, a recognition that meant a shattering of the idols or distorted images of God created by man.

All sin is a form of idolatry, making some created self-satisfaction one's supreme good (*summum bonum*) for the moment. In the sinful history of the individual and of the community this self-seeking and the projection of selfish desires and needs take on a concrete and (in the case of a religious person or culture) religious form. The false gods of Israel's neighbours frequently seemed irresistible to the Israelites precisely because they reflected these self-centred desires and needs. And even where no formal religious substitute for Yahweh emerges he is himself either distorted to meet these needs by the self-consciously religious, or ignored by the non-religious whose 'idolatry' is one of power or money or sex. Both the religious and the non-religious idolatries enter into the very structure of all human community so that the individual person who can come into existence and develop only in some community is necessarily and continually affected. He has a permanent need of repentance.

The most tragic cases of idolatry are always those of the religious people who pride themselves on their knowledge of and fidelity to the one true God. And the most tragic recorded instances of this appear in the gospel accounts of the Pharisees. Their self-righteous insistence on their knowledge of Yahweh was only matched by their abject failure to recognise Jesus Christ whom he had sent. They appear in the written word of God as a perpetual challenge to all religious leaders, to all religious people to examine how far they have substituted their own idea of god for the God of Abraham, of Moses, of Jesus Christ and of all men, and how they are in need of repentance.

Repentance then implies destruction of our idols, of our distortions of God. This destruction is necessarily painful because the idols are our own creation. In creating them we insulate ourselves against the true demands of reality. We erect protective barriers which will enable us to bask in our own selfishness and to encounter others only in so far as we need them and can use them. Repentance would dismantle these barriers and make us adjust to reality.

This adjustment to reality, always painful in itself, becomes particularly so when the reality is another person. Objects we can cope with. They are there, and their presence must be recognised and allowed for if one is to go on living. To ignore brick walls, steep ravines, an oncoming car or food for the body, is readily understood to be foolish and dangerous. To recognise them and cope with them does not normally involve any great personal decision. Persons and personal presence are quite different. The person, unlike the piece of furniture, cannot be simply dealt with, used or accepted in the same detached way. To do so is to fail to recognise the truly personal quality of the presence. It is to turn the person into an object, to exploit him for one's own satisfaction. It is even at the strictly human level a form of idolatry as a distortion of the true mystery of reality. Man frequently fails other persons in this way. The realisation that he has failed is born of an awareness of the true dimension of personal presence. It forms the beginning of that adjustment to reality called repentance and always carries its own pain.

Faith as the Beginning of Repentance

When failure to recognise the demands of personal presence is transposed to the level of the divine presence to man, its depth and the radical character of the adjustment required stand fully revealed. The adjustment itself depends on the continuing, loving presence of God which gradually awakens the sinner to some awareness that he is in this presence. The adjustment or return would not be possible if this presence were simply withdrawn. So repentance is a gift or a grace, the gift of God's loving presence seeking an entry into the sinner's heart. The first awareness of that presence initiates the first movement of return. The awareness itself is faith, as the recognition of God in his personal self-giving to man. It is the faith which in the words of Trent constitutes the root and basis of all justification or return to God (DS 1532).

For the sinner this recognition of God's loving presence is at first a source of distress and confusion. His temptation is to evade it. Few people can easily face a person they have injured in some way without seeking to distort the situation or the other person as a way out of their pain. The more intimately linked they are with this person, the more painful the presence becomes. Man's link with God occurs at the deepest level of his being. The presence of God to him emerges in that most intimate sphere of his own presence to himself. For God who dwells in man and is the source of his being (the immanent God) is yet beyond him (the transcendent God), challenges him to go beyond himself and so makes him aware of himself at the very core of his being. Awareness of failure at this level can be the most painful of all.

This awareness is possible through the persistent initiative of God in his loving presence. So it was for the Israelites in their chequered history as well as for the individuals encountering the living God in the person of Jesus Christ, for Mary Magdalen, Peter and the good thief. And the failure to repent of Chorazin and Bethsaida (*Matt.* 11:21; *Luke*

10:13) was culpable failure to recognise this divine presence in Jesus.

With Jesus the divine self-giving to men in love received its full visible and historical expression. This expression is continued in his Church. The loving presence of God at the core of each man's being receives its proper visible and historical expression in the Church. Repentance or conversion, the response of the sinner to God breaking through his self-imposed barriers, is duly and fully manifested in conversion to Jesus in his Church. Faith as personal awareness of God's presence becomes truly itself as Christian faith and for the sinner initiates that movement of return called penance. When the sinner like the prodigal son 'comes to himself', and reflects on his father's home the return journey has already begun (*Luke* 15:11ff.).

Continued in Hope

The distress at finding oneself in the presence of the God whom one has failed could decline into hopelessness or despair where this presence is not correctly understood as a loving and therefore forgiving presence. The bitter realisation of one's own failure must be balanced by this assurance of God's love and forgiveness. The first faltering movement of return in faith receives further impetus in the hope of forgiveness for past failures and of divine support in future difficulties. The dynamics of repentance (cf. *S. theol.* III, 85) take over as the divine presence draws hope out of faith and leads the sinner further on the road back. If over-concentration on one's own failure and lack of attention to the loving presence of God may drive the sinner further away through despair, no less dangerous are the casual dismissal of one's sins and the superficial presuming of divine forgiveness now or in the future. Presumption is not a development of faith but a distortion of it, turning the true God into a weak creditor to whom one will attend presently. The self-blinding that goes with presumption makes genuine recognition of the divine

G

presence and response to it inevitably harder for the future.

Completed in Charity

The movement of return begun in faith and sustained through hope reaches its completion in the (re)union with God called charity. In charity the loving presence of God to man becomes a loving union of man with God. Penance describes the dynamic movement of faith through hope to charity for sinful man. The self-gift of God to man in his sin provokes awareness of this continued loving presence. It provides the attractive force which lifts man out of his self-imposed isolation in sin and carries him forward to meet his forgiving Father (*Luke* 15).

All this is, of course, a gift of God, a grace. Repentance is not possible without grace (DS 1521, 1551). And what is primarily in question is what is called uncreated grace, God's gift of himself. Too frequently grace and its effects tend to be fragmented through failing to recognise the simple central reality, God himself giving himself to man in love, making man aware in various ways of this loving presence. From God's point of view grace is simply God himself, or God speaking to man, addressing man, loving man—all different ways of describing his giving himself to man, of his entering into a relationship with man which not only demands man's response but enables man to make it. Man can only love at God's level because God first loves him (1 *John* 4:10). He can make a personal response to God because God speaks personally to him. In speaking to him at his own level, in loving him at this level, God changes him. This is grace, the new life which man enjoys as a gift because it is a personal relationship with God made possible by God's gift of himself, by God's love, which is God (1 *John* 4:16).

Seen from man's point of view, the response which is at once demanded and made possible is an awareness of God's self-gift in love. It is a recognition of God as personally addressing man (faith) which develops under the divine power of attraction into the desire and trust (hope) necessary to man's complete self-giving (charity). Where man is inhibited in his awareness of God by personal and racial failure greater expression is demanded on God's part. And there could be no greater expression than the gift of his Son who laid down his life for men and whose first articulation of his own mission to men was to repent and believe the gospel or the good news of God's saving presence and love.

A Permanent Task

For sinful man the union in love with God is achieved only through repentance or return. And this is a painful (penitential in the popular sense) task. It is also a permanent, historical task. For mankind as a whole the task of repentance has a history coextensive with that of sin, stretching from the first refusal of God's personal offer to the last. And it remains necessary for mankind in the Christian as in the pre-Christian era. The total response of the man Jesus provides the model and the energy for the response of all others but they have to make this model and energy their own. It is a matter of human experience as well as divine revelation that nobody achieves this to perfection. All have sinned and continue in some degree to fail in their recognition of and response to the Father of Jesus Christ as the one true God.

Repentance, especially when it is described as conversion, has a once for ever air about it. At any rate it should be regarded as an unusual occurrence for somebody who has achieved first justification or conversion through faith and baptism. The image projected is one of a rather dramatic turn-about (*con-versio*) which could hardly be taken seriously if it were a frequent occurrence. In one very important sense this image of repentance is correct. The first reunion between the individual person born into a sinful condition and his God in baptism or through personal faith, hope and charity without baptism, has all these dramatic overtones.

So have any subsequent returns after serious breaches in the relationship through serious personal sin. How frequent such serious breaches may be for any single individual cannot, of course, be established *a priori* (and with very great difficulty and approximately *a posteriori*). What is clear is that man's historicity plays a real part in both the lapses and the reunions. The loss or gain of grace, of God's friendship, may be from one point of view instantaneous. From another important view point the lapse and return have their own history, because in Catholic theology they have a real human dimension (DS 1525, 1554). They involve the free collaboration of man and a real transformation of him. Both these must take place in history if they are to take place in man.

The dramatic conversion to God and no less dramatic departure from him may have their drama well concealed in the slow process of time. At any rate some time, however brief, is required for both. And it is more realistic to consider mortal sin, for instance, not as an isolated and instantaneous act but as the culmination of a process, a process of gradual neglect and distortion of the one true God which reaches flashpoint, perhaps, in some critical action that realises and manifests the full rejection of God which had been gestating over a period. Similarly the repentance is a process of gradual return under the influence of the loving presence of God in the manner described which reaches its climax in a critical action of genuine love of God.

The whole Christian life must be seen in this historical perspective, waxing and waning through periods of growth and periods of regression. The Christian from his first recognition and union with the Father in Christ faces the life-long task of growing in the recognition and in the union. The recognition of the seven-year-old is no longer adequate to the fourteen-year-old. The 'God' of elementary education may easily become a 'false God' at university level. New intellectual horizons and constant new experience demand constant revision and growth in our knowledge of God.

Knowing the one true God makes permanent demands on man because of his historical nature. It is only through his own personal history that any man can come to that knowledge (and love) of God to which he is called. In the sinful condition of man his knowledge of God is constantly threatened and continually obscured and distorted by his sinful tendencies. False Gods or at least false ideas of the one true God are man's permanent temptation. Knowing the one true God as a life-task becomes a never-ending battle with the subtle modifications and consequent distortion of God to which sinful man is prone. For some people there will be dramatic lapses and returns but for all there must be constant growth in knowledge of God which involves the continuous stripping away of these parasitic distortions which tend to smother the true belief in God. All men are sinners (*Rom.* 5:12) and have need of repentance. They continue to be sinners on earth and so repentance is a permanent demand which affects all men at all stages of their lives.

A Community Task

Man's permanent need of repentance at the individual and at the community level is powerfully illustrated in the official history of God's dealings with the people of Israel in the books of the Old Testament. God's definitive and irrevocable choice of this people as his people in the Mosaic covenant never met with parallel fidelity from the people. They constantly violated the covenant by worshipping false gods either explicitly in the Baalim of their neighbours or implicitly in their making various human satisfactions into their supreme good of the moment and one of the many strange gods they placed before Yahweh. The history of the people and its leaders became a divine call to repentance in action to match the divine call in word of the prophets, of Isaiah, Jeremiah and the rest.

With the establishment of the new covenant and the emergence of the new people of God the threat of the false gods did not automatically disappear. The achievement of Jesus in reconciling God with man and in ensuring through the gift of the Spirit that the knowledge and presence of the one true God continue in the people called the Church of Christ, provides for all men at all times a (certain) guaranteed visible link with God. Yet that link may be more or less effective in the world. It will be less effective if, as is bound to happen to some extent, the people who form the Church have by their sins distorted, at least implicitly, the knowledge of the one true God. It is not only by what they say about God but also by how they live, that the knowledge and love of God is mediated through the Church to the rest of men. At no time in the Church's history has what men say about God and what knowledge of him involves been so in harmony with the indwelling Spirit that there was no possibility of misunderstanding for men of goodwill. From the first 'Judaising' disputes amongst the apostles themselves through a succession of controversies, councils and heresies down to a particularly acute modern problem like that of contraception, the human limitations of the Church have inhibited the fuller manifestation of the Spirit. This is even more true of the witness of Christian living. Despite the example of the Christian heroes, the saints, the Church has in her leaders and people sometimes given much less effective testimony to the God of Jesus Christ than she should.

All this is to be expected. The gift of the Spirit and the guarantee of Jesus do not automatically eliminate human opacity or human sin. The recognition of such failure and of the constant threat of it, reinforces the Church's understanding of its lowly, pilgrim condition. The Church is a people on the way to God and that way is for Christians as for all men a way of return. The call to repentance applies now and always to Christians, not simply as individuals but as a community. (They are never simply individuals.) The current renewal or *aggiornamento* in the Church should not be seen as something unusual but as part of the Church's permanent need to do penance, to purify her understanding of her Lord, to destroy the false understanding which so easily becomes incarnate in her human traditions and laws. To fulfil her Christian witness in the world, as the community of love and so of God, the Church must continually do penance.

Penance is not merely a historical or enduring necessity for men, called for at all stages of his history. It is also a community necessity. Truly human activity is community activity. This is confirmed and deepened in the Christian understanding of God's relationships with man. He always addresses man in and through a community (Israel, the Church) and expects him to respond in and through a community. Man's response to God is at the same time a response to his neighbour and to the wider community. His failure towards God is at the same time a failure to his neighbour and to the community. Repentance and reconciliation are a return both to God and to the neighbour in community. The process of response through faith or recognition of God lovingly present, and hope or trust and confidence in God's forgiving and sustaining presence, leading to charity or the union in love with the loving God, has its neighbour-and-community-centred dimension too. A genuine recognition of the neighbour, going out to him in trust and union with him in love, forms a necessary accompaniment of return to God. The visible and effective Christian sign of return which is called the sacrament of penance is well seen as a reconciliation with the community and so with God.

A different aspect of community penance appears when one looks at failure *by* the community rather than *to* the community of the Church and its consequent need of repentance. But there are other communities and other community failures.

The problem of community or collective responsibility is a particularly tricky one and it cannot be discussed here. Yet it seems evident that many of the most glaring human failures in the world cannot be attributed to individuals and cannot be repaired or repented of by individuals. Individuals feel helpless in the face of world-hunger or war or religious, racial or class discrimination. Even much less critical national and local problems can appear beyond the efforts and therefore beyond the responsibility of the individual.

Because these problems can only be tackled at an organised community level, there is clearly community failure. As a first step to overcoming it, the community failure should be acknowledged and regretted. In this Christians should give a lead. One way of doing this would be to awaken the consciences of Christians to their failure by community exercises of repentance. The usual exercises in confession and missions or retreats remain in practice very individualist. The current renewal of the liturgy lays great stress on its community dimension. In some places this has already affected the practice of penance. What is in mind here is a public confession, on behalf of a particular branch of the community, of its failure at a community level, public expression of regret for this and public commitment to atoning for this failure. In this way various groups in the community could be awakened to their true Christian vocation and gradually liberated from their selfish class isolation into full community living. At this community level also penance is a necessary prelude to genuine Christian life and love.

From the Christian point of view the most scandalous failure in community is that of the Christian Churches amongst themselves. In their present search for unity and in response to their call to bear witness to the unity of all men in Christ, they could well give a lead in some ecumenical exercises of repentance where they would acknowledge their failures in a common service of prayer and sorrow and resolve to fight them for the future. As a stimulus to this they have the powerful example of Pope Paul at Vatican II asking pardon of the representatives of the other Churches present for any offences of the Catholic Church against them.

Virtue and Sacrament

The relation between penance and charity cannot be properly discussed without some brief reference to the relation between the virtue of penance and the sacrament. In the past there has been some confusion about this. It has even been suggested that there are two distinct ways of repentance or reconciliation (the Scotists), that of perfect contrition on its own (or an act of true charity) and that of attrition plus the sacramental absolution. This arises from a misunderstanding of the true nature of all Christian virtue and all Christian charity as derived from Jesus Christ, made visible and operative in the world through the Church (*das Ursakrment*) and the sacraments. All grace is Christian, ecclesial, sacramental, while at the same time demanding of the adult a personal response. The genesis of repentance through faith and hope to charity is ecclesial and sacramental whether the charity is given before the actual sacrament is received or whether the process which is still on the way and so imperfect, is actually completed in the sacrament. The process itself must always be completed by charity and this means integration into the ecclesial community which, unless there is some obstacle, should be externally expressed in the sacrament.

For fallen man repentance and charity belong together in a single dynamic movement of return to the Father. For man redeemed by the incarnation, death and resurrection of Jesus Christ, the act and virtue of penance are incorporated in that redeeming work and made a visible realisation of it in the sacrament.

6

Liturgy and Christian Living

For the Christian in the world today, one of his most urgent
needs in the attempt to do justice to both poles of his existence is an understanding of the relation of his activity in
the liturgy to his daily living. Although theology and
homiletics have always concerned themselves in some way
with the problem, there is evidence of a new crisis in this
area. The present preoccupation with 'religionless Christianity' inevitably liturgy-less, is one indication of this. The
long overdue reforms in the shape of the liturgy have not
realised the social hopes set on them. In both these critical
points what is at issue is the relation between liturgy and life.

My purpose here is to explore this relation. The approach
obviously cannot be that of the professional liturgist it must
be rather that of a theologian whose professional task is to
investigate the Christian revelation as a way of life it must
be that of the moral theologian—if such a being exists.

Trinitarian Shape

Liturgical prayer is said to be directed to the Father in
or through Christ the Son by the power of the Holy Spirit.
It has a trinitarian shape. Liturgy in the Christian Church
is a recalling and realising of the self-giving of the Son to
the Father made possible by the gift of the Spirit. This is
true supremely of the Eucharist but applies varying
degrees to the other sacraments and liturgical a What is

less commonly recognised is that the whole Christian life has this trinitarian shape. The call is to respond as son and brother in everything a man does. But the response of sonship is to the Father and this is only possible in Christ who constitutes the way for each. Sharing this way derives from the Spirit, sent as promised upon mankind in the Church and poured forth in the heart of each man so that he may be able to say with Christ, Abba, Father.

The Christian life expresses a relationship with each of the three divine persons. Every Christian activity realises and develops this relationship. The liturgy makes explicit what is implicit in all a Christian's activity. It attends formally to the underlying structure which gives its ultimate value to secular activity. Liturgy and life in this sense complement each other. The liturgy enables the Christian to interpret, express, and in a more fully human way accept the source and direction of his daily living. Daily living in turn provides in the incarnational context the opportunity to realise his ultimate destiny. It is as man, through the development of his humanity, that man after the manner of Christ is to realise his sonship of the Father.

Whatever we do is of value in so far as it is an expression of sonship of the Father. This applies equally to liturgical activity and to activity in the world. It provides the ultimate basis of the relation between liturgy and Christian living.

The Covenant

The God-man relationship has been formalised, as we have seen, in the covenant (*berith, diatheke, testamentum*). For Israel this was primarily the Mosaic covenant on Sinai. The agreements between Yahweh and Abraham or Noah or even Adam, recounted in the history of Israel and its origins, have the structure and force of a covenant also. The liturgical significance of the covenant for Israel can hardly be exaggerated. Liturgy was, in fact, a renewal of the covenant on Sinai and it is accepted that the accounts of that covenant which we have, derived from liturgical texts. The celebration of Yahweh's saving deeds by recalling them was an obvious way of honouring him and of pledging the people anew to the response demanded of them in virtue of the covenant. The covenant was at once a gift of Yahweh in making this people his people, and a demand for a response—that the people live as his people. It is in the setting of his covenanted choice that the Decalogue appears, summarising the way of life expected of his people. Liturgy and life as forms of fidelity to and renewal of the covenant were closely linked for Israel.

This is no less true of the 'new Israel' and the new covenant. Because the new covenant is realised not in an agreement, formally and externally expressed in the manner of the Mosaic one, but in the person, life, death and resurrection of Jesus Christ, both liturgical and living expression of it will be somewhat different. The liturgical celebration and renewal is not simply a recalling of the deeds of Yahweh in Jesus. It realises his covenant achievement in a way impossible for Israel and the Mosaic covenant. In the liturgy of the Christian Church the unique and all-sufficient response for man to the Father becomes available to men in effective sign. In the life of the Christian believer this same response of Jesus provides the model and the effective source of his every Christian activity.

The recent emphasis on the covenant dimension of the liturgy should be extended to the Christian life in general. The Christian life is a covenanted one. Its pattern determined by that new covenant which, according to Jeremiah, would be written on men's hearts. A serious moral action is a renewal or rejection of the covenant and the relationship it involves which the liturgical action formally and explicitly recognises.

Passover and Exodus

Related to the covenant aspect of the liturgy are the themes of Passover or Pasch and Exodus. The historical setting of these in the emergence of Israel as God's people made them obvious liturgical themes in the Old Testament. They have, however, received a deeper and more universal understanding in their application to the deeper and more universal achievements of God in Jesus Christ. Christians following the call of Jesus must follow him also into the unknown. They must, in fact, take up the cross and follow him through his death on the cross to the Father in resurrection and glorification. For Jesus and his followers the Passover and Exodus have taken the form of dying on the cross to rise to a new life. This new life constitutes the land of promise. Through the cross they are released from the Egyptian slavery of sin. They become the new people of God.

The liturgical expression of all this is well known. In the basic sacrament of baptism, as in the central sacrament of the Eucharist, the Exodus/Passover themes, in their Christian setting of sharing the death and resurrection of Jesus, predominate. The other sacraments by definition also express this central Christian mystery. But the response of Christian living as a following of Jesus and a participation in his sonship knows no other way than that of Jesus and his cross. In his situation in the world the Christian faces the challenge of serving God and neighbour by dying to himself and his own selfish interests. Christian love and service always involve this abandonment of self. It is born and develops in the shadow of the cross while in itself it is an expression of the new life and the freedom of the risen Christ. Each good moral decision involves a realisation, however slight, of the decisive self-giving of Jesus to his Father on the cross for mankind. The continuity between liturgy and life is fully confirmed here.

The Exodus/Passover theme and its Christian fulfilment reveal this continuity in a slightly different way when stress is laid on the journey aspect. The Exodus accomplished by Jesus is, in fact, shared with all men but it attains its fullness in them only at the end of their lives on earth. Life on earth assumes the form of a journey to this destination. They may have died together with Jesus to rise with him to a new life here as St Paul says, but they are still en route to where Jesus sits in glory. The route they have to follow is that of the Christian in the world. They cannot predict where exactly fidelity in following Jesus along this route may bring them. They are sustained like the Israelites by the presence of their God. And they have been provided with food for the journey. The journey remains a journey into the unknown. This applies to the precise when and where and how of the ultimate destination, but more relevantly here to the major decisions to be taken at various stages of the journey. Christian morality has suffered a great deal from the failure to recognise this venturing-into-the-unknown character of serious moral decision. The faith of Abraham has been replaced by a calculating prudence which fears nothing so much as the unknown. Such an attitude excludes almost any genuine Christian decision and the risk it inevitably involves. The true Christian goes forward trustingly in the half-light. The summons is not of his own choosing and the risk cannot be eliminated by any human calculation. It is in the liturgy that the ground of his daring is manifest and food for the journey assured.

The attempts to renew moral theology as a theology of the Christian life have naturally given pride of place to Christian love. As summarising the whole law it offers a single and simple guideline through the maze of contemporary moral problems. It enables the confused Christian to pick out the central virtue or quality which must characterise everything he does. (All this does not dispense with the need for hard moral analysis of how love is to be expressed in different areas and problems of Christian life, but it does make clear *what* is to be expressed.) Love eventually defeats all attempts at calculation in advance. As a gift of self to God and neighbour, no prior limit can be set to it. To love in Christian fashion is to sign a blank cheque. It is to leave the comfort of the known, the comfortable if enslaving known, for the hazardous but eventually liberating unknown. It is to take up one's cross and follow Jesus. He who loves after his example will no doubt suffer after his example. To love in his unconditional way is to be crucified. What is done sacramentally in memory of his death until he comes finds another expression in the love-life called Christian life.

The Community Context

Before examining some of the traditional dimensions of the liturgy such as worship, thanksgiving and petition in relation to Christian living, it is necessary to consider again the community aspect of both Christian liturgy and life. Liturgy as the work of a people or community has been, in the excitement of the recent renewal, vigorously contrasted with the individualism of private prayer. The long overdue reforms in the external shape of the liturgy have necessarily paid greater attention to fuller community participation and expression. The search for more satisfying forms which still goes on, with or without ecclesiastical approval, is very concerned with finding effective community expression. There might, however, be less anxiety about community expression if the community context of the liturgy were more fully understood. At least there would be no possibility of separating private prayer from liturgy as non-community. All Christian prayer, as a share in the response of Jesus to his Father, is community prayer. It is the prayer of a son who must also be a brother. In recognising their sonship of the Father men at the same time recognise their brotherhood of one another. The only-begotten Son alone has the right to say 'My Father'. Christians always pray, in public or in private, as the Lord himself taught them to pray, 'Our Father'. Unseen, private prayer is as Christian prayer also community prayer. The necessity and value of public expression of this community prayer in the liturgy should not obscure this community aspect of private prayer and its necessity and value. The attention and reflection which private prayer can develop will in turn deepen public expression of this same community reality.

The relation and contrast evident in the discussion of

private and public prayer is one aspect of the relation and contrast which pervades the whole existence of the Christian (and human) being. Christianity is a community reality. The contrast between individual and society as sometimes understood falsifies the true relation, better expressed in terms of person and community. Person and community are correlative terms. Man becomes a person in and through community. Community develops by the personal engagement and so development of its members. There is no personal activity that is not also a community activity. In Christian revelation this receives a deeper basis and more urgent dynamism. In becoming man God entrusted himself, after the pattern of all his revelation, to mankind and this gift is available to men in the community reality of the Church of Jesus Christ. For them this gift makes them sons of the Father and brothers of one another. Every Christian action like every Christian prayer is that of a son and brother. To be personal in the Christian, filial sense, it must be brotherly or open to the community, even if the immediate effects of this seem very slight.

Christian living, as I have shown in more detail earlier, is possible only in community. It can be understood only in community and is directed to the building of that final community of all men as sons of the Father and brothers of one another which is called the kingdom of God. The historical promotion of this forms the goal of all Christian activity in the liturgy or in the world. The particular contribution of the liturgy to the building of the human community, for so long neglected, is now in danger of being misunderstood. The anxious search for the most satisfying community form was in part due to a mistaken idea that the liturgy in some special and isolated way could be community forming. In fact, its function is rather that of expressing or making explicit the Christian community already in existence. And it can only express as much community as is there. Admittedly it expresses the underlying dimension of community which is given in Christ, and in doing so it makes accessible the ultimate springs of community life. But this gift is a challenge. The cosy feeling a particular liturgical celebration may give a particular group has nothing to do with real community. And the liturgy is no substitute for the daily task of building up the brotherhood of man. The enthusiasm which believes that of itself it will transform community living, lacks theological as well as empirical foundation. The forms ought to express as effectively as possible the community dimension of the liturgy but more important is how far there is any community for it to express.

Worship

The three traditional dimensions of liturgical activity I wish to consider here are: worship, thanksgiving and petition. This is not intended to dismiss others as of no consequence or to be a full-scale discussion of any of these. They have been selected as central to liturgy and as test cases for the distinction and continuity between liturgy and life. This test will naturally determine the limits of the discussion.

'Worship' has a mystifying air for most people. The usual, general definition is the acknowledgement of the excellence of another, in particular of God. The mental image associated with it for many people (mental images are frequently more powerful than definitions in the way people regard something), is of bended knees and bowed heads in an atmosphere of candles and incense before unreal figures in strange clothes. To say that one worships God conveys very little to the non-worshipper and sometimes even to the worshipper. The word is used too easily and frequently.

Some of this mystification would be removed if worship were understood as recognition and acceptance of reality, above all of the supreme reality of God. It is awareness of what is there, awareness of the Father as ultimate origin and destiny of all that man is and does. Awareness of reality at that depth does not come easily to man. It might be said (adapting T. S. Eliot) that a man can bear little worship

H

because he can bear very little reality. At any rate special occasions must be set aside to permit more attention to the ultimate reality. Yet the very notion of special occasions for worship can have unfortunate consequences for its true understanding.

The whole of life can be summed up in the words 'knowing the one true God and Jesus Christ whom he has sent'. It is a recognition of reality. Each good human act expresses this recognition. The bad human act or sin is a failure to recognise this reality of the one true God. In the biblical vision it is a form of idolatry, of the creation and worship of false gods. Sin is an unwillingness to recognise, in the personal and accepting sense, the reality that is there. It is a failure to worship. The 'worship' of daily living is continuous with that of the liturgy inasmuch as both are personal recognition by man of the supreme reality of God. The recognition which a man achieves in ninety-five per cent of his time in the world, is much more likely to determine his recognition at the liturgy than vice versa. The god predominating in his day-to-day living cannot be simply shed at the church door on Sunday. The real treason of the clerics is to accept, as they frequently do, the god created by society in protection of its power, property and comfort as the God of Jesus Christ. The predominant god is known not from the name on the lips of the liturgists but from the hearts' desire of the people concerned. It is too easy to worship God with one's lips but where a man's heart is, there is his God.

The liturgy as the making explicit of the worship expressed in daily living can, of course, and should enable the Christian to purify his idea of God. It offers the opportunity of return or repentance. Here it is possible to put aside the false gods and become aware again or open to the one true God. The human drive towards reality may again assert itself. And this is part of the function of all liturgy. For this reason an intelligible and vital form is very necessary.

There remains the danger, however, that this return will

be evaded and the weekly liturgy thought of as the price to be paid for a quiet conscience in service of the weekday gods. To keep up attendance at this weekly liturgy the priests may fail to announce the true God and allow the worshippers to carry on in their idolatry. The continuity between life and liturgy, true or false, does not allow it to be called anything else. Because all human activities are ambivalent, a mixture of good and bad, there will always be some element of idolatry in our liturgical practice. What is so disquieting so often is the amount, to judge from the toler-ance of social evil by ardent church-goers. It is not possible to recognise the one true God as Father on Sunday if one has failed to recognise one's true brother in Christ from Monday to Saturday.

Petition

Worship as an awareness and acceptance of reality is closely related to petition which has always been a feature of Christian liturgy and prayer. And the dangers are no less. Much of the prayer of petition is of a magical kind directed to a false god. This false god is a god of the gaps who is expected to intervene and supply for human or natural deficiency and frequently merely to satisfy one's own com-fort. Prayers for fine weather or success of one kind or another imply that God will show himself in some miraculous activity to displace the ordinary secondary causes. It may not appear so crudely in what is said or thought but that is what too often lies behind.

Prayer of petition is not so much prayer that God may hear man. He knows what man has need of before man asks him. It is rather prayer that man may hear him in the actual situation in which he is. It is prayer that he may discern and listen to God's voice especially in the cries of need of his neighbour. Too often prayers for peace, for example, are evasions of the reality because there is refusal to listen to God speaking through the world's hungry and deprived. Too often it takes some threat to one's own life or property before one becomes aware of poverty and oppression. One may be reluctant to accept the saying of Mao Tse Tung that freedom is born out of the mouth of a gun. Yet one is more impressed by the sounds from the mouth of a gun than by the sounds from the mouths of starving children. One is more sensitive to the sound of breaking glass than to the sound of breaking hearts. To pray for others in their misfortunes is Christian where it is seen as God summoning one to listen carefully and attend to their needs.

Thanksgiving

Thanksgiving so far characterises Christian liturgy that its central act bears that name—Eucharist. In the response of Christ men are able to say thanks to the Father for his loving kindness to them. To recognise God for what he is, is to recognise him as the source of all that a man has and is. All worship is in that sense thanksgiving. But then so is all Christian living and behaviour. Each human act, as a recognition of the self-gift of God, as a realisation of this gift in human Christian development, is a way of saying thanks. Unless a man uses his talents of nature and grace as fully as he can, he is not showing proper appreciation of them or being genuinely thankful to God.

Because all in the Christian life is grace or gift the continuing response must be gratitude. Life as a whole is a gift, the individual situation is a gift and the response is also a gift, so that there is nothing to do except to gratefully accept. In a more legalistic framework the Christian life and moral behaviour were seen as a form of self-salvation by one's own good works. Jesus' condemnation of the Pharisees or Paul's treatment of the works of the Law have been overlooked. A theology of the Christian life expressed in thanksgiving or eucharistic terms could prevent such a mistake.

Conclusion

The conclusion of these reflections is inescapable. Liturgy

and life are so closely bound together that they may never be considered separately without distorting one or other. Liturgy makes explicit what is implicit in the secular activity of the Christian. The same underlying relationship to the trinitarian God is given two different modes of expression.

It might seem that the liturgical expression is superfluous if not harmful by distracting from the 'real' expression of the relationship in daily living, especially in the service of the neighbour. This line is favoured by those who espouse 'religionless' Christianity. A more radical line still is that of the 'God is dead' movement or the Christian atheists. The whole Judaeo-Christian tradition of God's dealing with man rules out such a conclusion. In this tradition the underlying structure broke through the surface and could be seen for what it was. The breakthrough was completed only in Christ. In the liturgy the structure, fully manifest and realised in Christ, continues to break surface. It appears for what it is and is realised in sign. So one is consciously put in touch with the sources of daily living and enabled to interpret it correctly in the light of the revelation of Jesus Christ. It must be conceded to those that see no further use for liturgy that it has been abused to misinterpret the Christian message and to worship false gods where the continuity with the corrective of life has not been properly recognised. No doubt the gods of some kind of liturgical expression ought, by Christian standards, to have been dead long ago. Daily living has need in its turn of the meaning and power of the liturgy. Their complementary functions reflect the divine and human dimensions of the incarnate Son of God and of the destiny to which men are called in him. It is only in and through the human that the divine element can operate and achieve its fulfilment in this world. Yet for it to be known as divine it must break through normal human expression and give evidence of its presence. For the human dimension to be fully itself in the actual context of the mission of Christ it must be that of a son of the Father. It is the function of the liturgy to bear witness to this and so enable man consciously to achieve it. For this it will always be necessary. However, divorced from Christian living or in any way regarded as a substitute for it, liturgy tends to lapse into idolatry. Life and liturgy, in continuity yet distinct, have need of each other.

7

Christian Marriage in an Ecumenical Context

AT FIRST sight 'Christian Marriage' might seem a discouraging theme for ecumenical dialogue. There are such obvious and apparently deeply rooted divisions between the different Christian Churches that only long and expert discussion at a developed stage of the dialogue could hope to yield profitable results. Because it is something that touches everybody very nearly, sexual and marital morality is always in the news and the diverse Christian views are now common knowledge. The more popular of these debates concern mixed marriages, indissolubility and divorce, contraception and family-planning with abortion as a related theme and finally premarital and extramarital sex. There are other less popular but no less profound problems, like the sacramentality of marriage and its 'natural law' base, as well as the relation between marriage and celibacy.

The very 'popularity' of these discussions and the fact that they are of immediate personal concern to so many make it impossible to avoid them. The shortness of the time to deal with them is some handicap but then there will never be enough time and our task must be to use the time that is available to the best advantage. Nor is a lack of so-called expertise altogether a disadvantage. Once the ecumenical dialogue has become exclusive to experts it will be dead. And while the services of the experts are always necessary these services must be set in the wider context of the

Christian people in general groping and growing towards that unity to which Christ is summoning it. In matters so personal as sex and marriage the necessary services of the experts have more obvious limitations.

The way forward here as elsewhere is for each Church to seek a deeper understanding of its own theology of marriage by returning to its Christian roots, especially in Scripture. Such a theology, biblical in origin, has gone through a development in the course of history which has at once clarified it and obscured it; at once been faithful to the original Christian vision and, in some degree at least, betrayed it. The inherent dynamism of the Christian message, its capacity and need to speak to different ages and different problems make such development essential. A simple biblicism is a betrayal of the Bible. The promise of the Spirit ensures the indefectibility of the Church and guarantees a certain freedom from error in doctrinal formulation; it does not eliminate the possibility of human weakness and error. It does not prevent the silt of human history with its built-in ambiguity from cluttering up the channels of Christian tradition or muddying the waters. This inherent dynamism in Christian teaching and the threat of human failure make development and purification a constant task of the Church. In matters of sex and marriage this is no less true.

Within the Roman Catholic tradition Scripture has always provided the primary source for the theology of Christian marriage. Admittedly in some of the manual presentations this scriptural basis was not given the explicit treatment it merited, and as a result an over-legal picture of marriage as a contract emerged. Yet this too had its biblical background and the fuller biblical teaching continued to exercise an important influence, as the encyclicals of Leo XIII and Pius XI give witness. It was only in our own time, however, due to the biblical movement on the one hand and the fuller psychological understanding of person and sex on the other, that a comprehensive theology of marriage began to emerge. This is not to say that all the problems have been solved. Quite evidently not all those already recognised have been solved and what new ones the future may bring nobody can say. But a wider and more fully Christian framework has been uncovered within which the Church may work towards a solution of present and future problems.

This Christian framework is characterised by three key-points: creation, incarnation and glorification. They are key-points in every Christian discussion. Their particular relevance to the discussion of marriage is solidly grounded in the Bible and they provide a useful way of summarising the Roman Catholic viewpoint.

Creation

Biblical and Christian teaching on marriage must begin from the creation accounts in the book of Genesis. This is where the Bible as we have it begins but more important it is the reference point for the New Testament teaching of Jesus in the gospels and of the other writings.

The two accounts, the Yahwist (ch. 2) and the Priestly (ch. 1) as they are called, offer complementary pictures of marriage. In both accounts the origin of sex and marriage from God or Yahweh is stressed. As coming from God they are good, so the narrator frequently describes creation. As created, however, and by a God who was in Hebrew understanding non-sexual, they were human not divine realities. The Hebrew tradition avoided both distorted extremes in ancient attitudes to sex: the divinisation of it and the revulsion from it as evil. These two tendencies have never disappeared from the world and much of Christian thought on marriage has been elaborated in defence against one or other.

Created and so good, sex and marriage as presented in Genesis have a double role in human living as designed by God. In the earlier Yahwist account of chapter 2 the community of love which husband and wife form together emerges very clearly. Yahweh has created man as the climax of his creation of the animals but he is unable in all creation to find him a suitable companion. So from the side of man when he is asleep he takes a rib and builds it into a new being who is called woman. This being of the same nature as himself yet sexually different, man accepts with a song of delight and the unity of the two in one flesh is presented as closer and more radical than any other human union, for instance that of parents and children.

In chapter 1 the creation of man as sexually diverse is related closely to his creation in the image of God without, however, any of the pagan association of divine sexual activity. The emphasis on the image serves to highlight the superiority of man to the rest of creation in his sexuality as in all other respects. The direction in which the narrative moves, however, is to revealing the privilege and responsibility which the gift of sex involves for mankind: that of filling the earth and subduing it or carrying on the work of creation by bringing further images of God into the world and so organising the resources of the world in the service of man, humanising it.

Although the double aspect of community of love directed to new life in children comes through the Genesis stories, the Old Testament laid much greater stress on the aspect of offspring. Conscious of itself as the called people to whom and through whom salvation was to come Israel saw children as the main point of marriage. And it would be wrong to expect the personal consciousness of later times in the relations between the sexes. Yet the reality of sexual and marriage love was not confined to the creation narrative. The most striking treatment of it is undoubtedly that in the Song of Songs, a collection of lyrical love poems.

It is possible to recognise this love implied in the use by Hosea and others of the marriage relation as an image of the relation between Yahweh and his people. The fidelity and tender loving care which Yahweh displays to his bride Israel in face of infidelity must reflect some contemporary insight into human marriage as a bond of love.

There is no express systematic teaching on marriage available in the New Testament. At critical stages in the development of its teaching it refers back with approval to Genesis. This occurs when Jesus is questioned by the Pharisees on divorce. To the surprise of his questioners he subordinates the teaching of Moses to that of Genesis. For him marriage in creation was indissoluble and the later concession, he implied, no longer operated.

Incarnation

It is not his express teaching, however, that is of first importance in assessing the impact of Jesus on our understanding of marriage. What he was rather than what he said comes first. And he was the incarnate Son of God. In becoming man and inviting man in turn to share his sonship of the Father he disclosed a new dimension to human living. The God-man relationship fostered by God with his people Israel in the Old Testament reached a climactic stage when God actually became man. The distinction between God and man still to be carefully cherished is not enough to do justice to the new reality. In Christ men become sons of the Father, brothers of Christ, indeed members of Christ, temples of the Spirit and partakers in the divine nature.

Such startling revelations of the condition of man must have their effect on all the created dimensions of man. Their effect on human sexual love and marriage emerges in the deepening of sexuality already evident in the Sermon on the Mount. Adultery in the heart is to be avoided no less than the external kind. Paul takes this up, condemning such an act as making the members of Christ members of a harlot. And the reduction of the whole law to love of God and the neighbour demands that a man love his life as well as other people.

The depth and range of married love appears in the Letter to Ephesians. The depth and range is that of Christ for his Church. The former description of the love of Yahweh for Israel receives a new urgency and depth in 'the great mystery' of Ephesians 5. The self-giving love of Christ for his Church is manifest in and a challenge to the love of Christian husband and wife. The human bond becomes a sign and a realisation of the love of God for his people in Christ. It is a sign and realisation of grace in the accepted terminology of Catholic theology.

Glorification

With the incarnation and mission of Jesus the kingdom of God is already among us; the last days are here. In the risen Lord the final consummation of man and his world has been achieved. Yet that consummation is not yet everyman's. The kingdom or reign of God has not been extended in its fullness to all creation. The last days may still encompass many years. We live in that in-between stage when what is in Christ must yet be completed for us.

The orientation which this waiting for glorification gives to Christian living in general affects Christian marriage also. Indeed in 1 Corinthians Paul wrestles with this very problem in a way that seems to place the whole value of marriage in question according to some commentators.

Jesus adverted to the peculiar situation of marriage in the fullness of the kingdom, when he answered the Sadducees about the rightful husband of a woman who married a number of brothers successively in accord with the Law. 'For when they rise from the dead they neither marry nor are given in marriage but are like the angels in heaven' (*Mark* 12:25).

It is in the light of the inbreaking kingdom that marriage is to some extent relativised in the New Testament. For all the transformation it undergoes as sign and bearer of Christ's love for his Church, it belongs in a real sense to the passing form of this world. And with the actual coming of the Messiah the posterity of Abraham has achieved its purpose and marriage is no longer the only way of discharging one's duty to increase God's people. Admission to the new world is by spiritual birth at baptism. For the sake of the kingdom, then, men may sacrifice marriage. Celibacy or 'becoming a eunuch for the kingdom of God', after the example of Christ and Paul, was recognised from the beginning as an appropriate Christian vocation and it was seen as reflecting in a special way the yet-to-be-fulfilled aspect of Christianity. Possible in the aftermath of the incarnation, celibacy not only allowed a certain kind of freedom in serving the kingdom, it served above all as a visible reminder of our unfulfilled state. As a way of life it called attention forcibly to the glory beyond.

The goodness of marriage, its created and incarnated goodness, has always merited the special defence of the Christian Church against the attacks of Gnostics, Manichees, Cathars, Jansenists and the like. No Christian age has been completely free from such attacks and it would be too much to expect that Christian understanding should not have suffered in the process. So much of the Catholic teaching on marriage has been developed in reaction to error that it has from time to time shown the unbalance of reaction. This was most obvious recently in an overlegal presentation but also in a rather unreal estimation of celibacy with some consequent devaluation of marriage. Just now, to judge by the public discussion, we are reacting towards the opposite extreme. In the rounded Christian picture of creation, incarnation and glorification, marriage and celibacy complement each other. Marriage is the more usual vocation but that is not in any way to cheapen it. It is a way of perfection for a man and wife with a special Christian role in the world, testifying to the love of Christ for us all by showing human love at its most intense and intimate as the bearer of the divine love. It testifies to the value of creation in itself and to its transformation by the incarnation. Celibacy, while not denying but sacrificing this created, incarnated good, testifies to the final stage of glorification which awaits this and all other human goods in resurrection with Christ.

Comparison between the states is neither necessary nor helpful; both are ways of perfection for those who are called to them.

The traditional qualities of Christian marriage belong within this framework of creation, incarnation and final glorification. Already in the creation stories exclusiveness and permanence are demanded. It is by the union of one man and one woman that the unity in one flesh which cannot be broken is achieved. This is certainly the meaning which Jesus ascribes to it. The love in this sense is exclusively directed to the other and the commitment born of that love is forever. Only a love so permanent and exclusive does full justice to the created reality described in Genesis or to the transformed reality of the Letter to the Ephesians. Only such a relation could bear witness and realise the love of Christ for his Church.

This in brief is the Roman Catholic view of the theology of marriage as outlined, for example, in its latest treatment of the subject at the Second Vatican Council. The pastoral constitution of that Council, The Church Today, devotes chapter I of Part II to 'Marriage and the Family'. The older legal framework with its hierarchy of ends is dropped and marriage is presented as a community of love directed to new life.

It would be a serious mistake to regard a theological and necessarily abstract framework, however true to the data in creation and revelation it may be, as providing a complete picture of Christian marriage or as offering a ready answer-book for present and future problems. There is a real temptation, especially for unmarried theologians, to roman-ticise marriage in an unreal (and therefore unloving) way as a community of love when many marriages palpably are not. Here it is very important to keep in mind what is true of all Christian realities, that they are merely on the way to becoming what they are in principle, that is, in Christ. Marriages have to be made by the parties involved and that can only mean that they have to be made loving.

Many marriages are, as we say, problem, if not loveless, marriages because the couple received little or no help in preparing for marriage and still less towards meeting the difficulties which inevitably arise within it. In an ecumenical context we should show our common Christian concern for the married by considering how we might co-operate to offer the best possible pre-marriage courses and post-marriage counselling services to all our people. Co-operation might take varying forms and degrees but I am quite sure that our problems are basically the same and our resources equally limited, so that a pooling of them would be of real value. It would in addition give that practical outlet to our aspirations for unity which we need so badly. Practical co-operation is not ruled out any more than dialogue because of the differences I listed briefly at the beginning of this chapter. These do, of course, limit but not necessarily to the extent that some people believe.

The question of divorce and indissolubility need not be so divisive when it is remembered that the Christian Churches we know uphold indissolubility in principle, that every responsible Christian is interested in preserving marriage and the family and not in easy dissolution and that in every Church tradition there is found dissolution of already validly existing marriages. The strong Roman Catholic commitment to the indissolubility of marriage is shared in differing degrees by all Christian Churches. The differences are of degree and sometimes very slight degree. In preparing people then for mature marriages and in assisting with a threatened breakdown within marriage serious Christians who share the same problems and the same goals ought to consider sharing their resources.

Family regulation is another area in which there is an unnecessary amount of misunderstanding. The goals, whether expounded by the Lambeth Conference or the Vatican Council, are the same, the achievement of that family for which the parents can provide in a responsible way, considering their total situation. The means do cause division. The Roman Catholic Church has so far accepted only one means, abstinence, periodic or complete, as preserving the creational values of human sexuality, and has clearly ruled out abortion or its extension, infanticide. The area between has been the subject of special study and it would be only fair to ask other Christian bodies to respect the difficulties of such a situation. Roman Catholics in turn must respect the position of other Christians in a matter so delicate. At the level of educating towards the goals of family planning there is much room for co-operation. Honest discussion in charity could be of help also in espousing the most human and effective means.

Premarital and extramarital sex are regarded as further danger zones. Roman Catholics are naturally alarmed by popular versions of the Quaker report on these matters or the more recent one of the British Council of Churches' Commission. Again distinctions must be made between the views of Churches and the views of particular individuals or groups. The Quaker report was certainly of this latter kind. And what is upheld objectively or in principle must be distinguished from what is tolerated subjectively or as an exception. Some of the most critical and criticised interventions on the 'concessive' side have at least posed real questions for the rest of us and given us no alternative except to develop a sexual ethic which incorporates the inherited wisdom of Christianity with the psychological, social and other insights of our own time. In pursuit of this the collaboration of all the Christian Churches is clearly desirable.

The sacramentality of marriage appears much less divisive in the renewed Catholic understanding of the sacraments. Sign and realisation of God's self-giving to men in Christ, a sacrament is not a thing which can be employed magic-wise to produce some infallible effect. It involves a personal response by men to the personal offer of Christ. Not all sacraments signify or realise this dialogue between God and man in the same way. For some Christians the inability to see marriage as a sacrament precisely in the sense of the Eucharist or baptism leads them to reject the Catholic position. . . . But Catholics do not see all the sacraments as enjoying precisely the same mode of sacramental being. The well-known difficulties in analysing a number of the sacraments, including marriage, into matter and form on the classical models of baptism and Eucharist are ample proof of that.

The bugbear which natural law and its role in understanding marriage proves for many Reformation Christians might be removed if the discussion were carried on in different terms. The terms used in this chapter, those of creation, may not be acceptable to all. They have the advantage, however, of being biblical. The terms are not important if agreement could be reached about what is really under discussion—the human endowment of sexuality and then the human-Christian situation in which it has to be lived. Many earnest defenders of the genuine truth in the natural law teaching did themselves a great disservice by ignoring the more sophisticated approach of Aquinas, who refused to consider it as a code or book of instruction which could be fully written down and was unchangeable for all time. Aquinas may have lacked a historical sense such as we have today but he was not so naive as to believe that no distinctions should be made within the recognised obligations of natural law or that the less central ones would not change with changing circumstances. For the modern Catholic theologian natural law morality belongs within the more comprehensive moral theology centred in Christ, who in himself sums up the way to human perfection as at once Son of the Father and man. The human in all its historical, social, personal and so sexual dimensions has been established in Christ as the manner of realising divine sonship.

Despite the slight progress made by the statement from Rome in 1966 and that of the Synod of Bishops, October 1967, the problem of mixed marriages remains the most divisive in this field. While it awaits further theological clarification and the improved ecumenical climate which would make that possible, we must not allow ourselves to be hypnotised by the problem to the extent of ignoring the real opportunities for co-operation. Co-operation in other areas connected with marriage will do much to create the climate and foster the understanding necessary to the solution of this problem.

With a common framework based on the Bible and their Christian heritage, and with a common pastoral concern, the divided Christian Churches may come closer together in seeking to share ideas and pool resources in face of their common problems about Christian marriage. The well-known obstacles to full unity in this work should not be allowed to prevent them here any more than in other areas from doing what can be done and leaving the final unity to the movement of the Spirit.

8

Christian Marriage Today

THE TITLE of this chapter is in some ways misleading.
Marriage basically is a *human* institution; we may obscure
it by adjectives, even adjectives as distinguished as 'Christian', but it is a human institution which is in a *continuing*
stage of development, so that there is no day or time of
day when one can stop and say, 'This is Christian marriage
at 8 p.m. on such-and-such a day!' It isn't like that because
it is a human institution; a human institution with a
Christian meaning; a human institution that is the bearer
of divine energy in the world—but yet a human institution.
As such it has a history, a history which goes back as it were
into a pre-history, into an era where we have little or no
records of the kinds of relationships within which men and
women lived, in which they continued the race and continued
to love one another. A developing changing institution in
its Christian meaning; we have in recent years acquired
some new ideas concerning that Christian meaning—some
of them conflicting ideas. It is important to remember this
point in analysing our situation at present; that marriage
is human first of all and then a bearer of certain divine
power or energy in the world. It is because we have forgotten
the historical changing character of marriage, because we
have mistaken one particular form, one particular realisation
of this marriage and called that Christian marriage, that
we are sometimes unable to see through our difficulties today.

These difficulties are fairly well known, but I do believe that if we had a more historical attitude to this human institution some of them might have been avoided. C. S. Lewis remarked that he who ignores history is the prisoner of history, the prisoner, then, of recent history; and because we have ignored history in some aspects of marriage we now find ourselves in rather serious difficulties. Marriage has changed, is changing and will continue to change. Our Christian understanding of it will continue to change. We have to live with that change. The difficulty of course lies in distinguishing true and false change; not every development is a genuine true human development and bearer of divine power or energy or love in the world. But there is development.

At the moment we are greatly taken up with one particular aspect of marriage in which development has been taking place: that is the aspect of responsible parenthood and the regulation of birth. Development has taken place in Christian thinking and in our particular Church in this matter; quite far-reaching development, and of course it would be foolish to think that the development is over. However, we have tended to become obsessed with just one particular aspect of this problem, the *method of birth regulation*—that is, the means whereby we exercise responsible procreation, and this obsession has distorted our view of marriage and our discussion of the problem. It would be idle to deny that this problem, despite authoritative pronouncements, despite the most learned theological arguments, has not been solved. And it would be foolish to expect that it will be solved in the near future. I do not intend to dwell on this problem but to try to open up other aspects of marriage where I see growth and development are taking place. Here it is possible to see how the human institution may be developed for releasing divine energy in the world, and so perhaps later on if these ideas are followed out, this particular problem, however urgent and hard for many people, may eventually find a solution.

As a human institution marriage has in our recent understanding come to be seen particularly as a relationship, a
personal relationship. Theology may be faulted for its late
discovery of this aspect of marriage, but theology and
theologians are dependent for their understanding of human
institutions on the way these institutions develop and the
way other people, people other than theologians, think
about them and present them. Above all, celibate theologians
are very dependent on the experience and reflection of
married people if they are to conduct some kind of dialogue
between this human institution and the word of God which
it is to bear, to carry, to show forth. There has been a
belated recognition among theologians of the deeply and
truly personal character of the marriage relationship. Yet it
was always there in the history of theological thinking, in
the New Testament, in St Augustine, in St Thomas, and it
was very much there in *Casti Connubii* where it was pointed
out that the primary reason or ground of marriage was in
fact this love-relationship between the couple.

The development therefore is not due primarily to
theologians but to theologians reflecting on the secular
reality which they saw about them and which they had to
come into contact with in trying to understand the word of
God. This interchange between the word and the world in
which we live, which it is the task of the theologian to work
on, reflect on, bring out, has shown us how much marriage
has emerged as a personal relationship. But this personal
relationship has to be understood from a number of angles
which may have been neglected.

First of all it is a personal sexual relationship. This is
fairly obvious. This personal sexual relationship between a
man and a woman enables them to communicate at a whole
series of levels, and then at that very profound and total
level that we consider sexual intercourse. However, it is
important to see their communication not simply as sexual
intercourse but as a man-woman communication in the
whole of their lives; in every minute of their lives they have

been acting as man and woman, as husband and wife. The sexual act itself as the profound radical expression of their love can be at once the richest human expression, and at the same time that which manifests most clearly and most effectively the divine energy or divine love in the world. But all the other expressions, sexual love expressions, are important and they form a continuing, continuous reality which enables husband and wife to grow together.

In this sexual communication which distinguishes the marriage as a personal relationship we are apt to forget that the rest of us are also sexual beings. We are apt to forget that there are beings who are not married and who are yet sexual and can communicate only as sexual beings. We are apt to forget above all, perhaps, single people who in all their lives must and do enjoy personal relationships and do so, not in spite of their sexual endowment, but in and through it as men and women. And if we would understand the sexual communication of marriage we have to understand the much wider range of sexual communication that goes on in the world between men and men, women and women, men and women; that we react and interact with one another out of our sexual character as masculine or feminine. This applies not simply to single people in the sense we normally think of single people, but also of course to celibates or people within religious life, and they again have to express their own sexuality and recognise that the expression of their love for people (and they must be loving people if they consider themselves Christians) will involve their sexual endowment as men or women.

We have tended therefore to think of sexual communication as either confined to marriage or, even within marriage, confined to sexual intercourse, and we have forgotten that we are always reacting and acting as sexual beings. We have tended to define chastity in a negative way as abstention from all sexual acts outside marriage, and then to be quite puzzled about what it could mean in marriage except that we rule out some other forms of action. Whereas of course chastity is our progressive liberation, whether as single, celibate or married, whereby our sexual powers are co-ordinated in an appropriate way so that we can communicate fully as persons with other people in this situation. Chastity then is not a negative thing in either single people or married. Chastity is not either something that is simply given and for most of us may be lost by some accident or other. Chastity is something we acquire as we endeavour to co-ordinate and harness our sexual endowment in the service and love of other people.

Marriage then is not the only sexual relationship, or the only state in which people exist as sexual beings and in which there may and must be fulfilment.

Secondly, marriage is sometimes treated as a personal relationship so isolated from others that the husband and wife become some kind of nuclear reality cut off from the rest of the world. This is perhaps to be attributed in theory at any rate to a romanticising of how much one person can fulfil the needs of another. Marriage as a personal relationship exists in a net work of relationships. It exists in community. Husband and wife normally have a whole network of relationships within which they must grow and develop together, and which they may not deny, which they naturally take into marriage with them, some of which they acquire with each other in marriage itself. It is one personal relationship among others; a very particular one, a unique one as far as two people are concerned, and yet not an isolated one, because, for one thing, if they are turned in on one another in an isolated way, they may not be able to bear the burden or the strain of being thus isolated. For another thing, in so far as they are enriching each other, in so far as they are developing through their love of each other, that love ought to be outgoing and enriching the community to which they belong. A self-centred two-in-one love in fact is failing in its relationship to other people and is generally diminishing if not destructive of itself.

Further, this personal relationship is not something that takes place once for all, or comes into being at a certain moment before an altar by exchange of consent. Marriage is something that is always in the making. It is not something that one can ever speak of as a finished article. It is a process; because all of us are unfinished articles, all of us are in the process of becoming ourselves, of realising the possibilities and potentialities which we have. Our realising of our possibilities and potentialities depends by and large on our interaction with other people. This means that marriage itself, the closest, most unique interaction that we know, must be ever in the process of development. This process of development is never completed, and it raises interesting questions about the stages through which it may pass. It sometimes happens that people enter into some such relationship which seems to be leading to marriage. The relationship may even reach something like the engagement stage, and then collapse. Clearly the relationship which had developed, began at a certain stage to disintegrate and this became progressively known to the people involved, luckily before they had exchanged consent. But one would also have to ask the question in some cases where in fact the relationship had begun to disintegrate, when had the couple begun to move apart, and if through force of circumstances they went through the form of marriage so that formally they were married whereas in fact the relationship had broken down before this—one would have to ask whether there was a real marriage here or not.

The process of marriage—which as I have said is always in the making—is, like ourselves and all our relationships, in the making in so far as it is being directed to something beyond itself, in so far as it is challenged by some future or some other reality which calls this couple out of themselves so that they develop in this way. And this is what is so specifically characteristic of marriage, that it has built into the relationship as it were a challenge or a call to go beyond itself; a call to go beyond itself in the procreation of children and a call then through the children themselves for the husband and wife, now become parents, to move out and beyond themselves in order to serve the children. Every relationship, then, is directed beyond itself to the wider community. Marriage has a particular kind of beyond which belongs to it—the beyond of the possibility of procreation and then the fact of family. And it is here again one of the sources of growth. So that while the transformation or move from being husband and wife to being parents may create some difficulty, and this sometimes can be critical in a family, it is precisely when presented with this challenge that the husband and wife move into a new stage of development in the relationship which is then directed beyond itself.

This specific character of marriage as that relationship which finds its fulfilment beyond itself, in new centres of love and life which we call children, is the expression or fruit of the relationship, the love of husband and wife. And while we are still groping, both intellectually and in every other sense, for a way of helping people to live or realise this in the fullest human form possible, we do realise now that the direction of marriage is not towards the largest possible family and not towards the smallest we can get away with, but towards that family appropriate to each particular couple. And this of course will change with themselves as they develop; so it would very likely be impossible for them to say on the day they get married that they will have two children, because that's suitable to them. Indeed they may be unsuitable for having any children whatever and not for physical reasons. But this direction towards children cannot be specified towards any particular number; all one can say is that it must be sought both in procreation and in the consequences which we call education, in as responsible and as human a way as possible. And this is the primary goal in marriage, not primary in the sense that it comes before the relationship but one which arises immediately out of the relationship, specifying it, and comes before the particular question of the means by which this is to be realised. So we do not therefore allow ourselves to be diverted from the more important, the realisation of the best family possible, to the less important, the particular means—however important they may be in themselves.

All this takes account of the character of marriage as a human institution, as a developing institution with different patterns in the history of society. In our own society, even in our lifetimes, we are aware of different patterns of how marriage is made and lived; of how it comes into being and continues to exist. We are aware that it still happens, and perhaps for some good reasons, that marriages are still arranged in some places. We are also aware that there is a pattern of marriage-making that is related to the process of choosing one's own partner, which is more or less romanticised into falling in love. We are aware then of a change, and different patterns of marriage coming into existence in our own country and society. And if we step out of our society into the world we find a very large range of pattern of how marriage comes into existence. Similarly with regard to the living of marriage there are very different patterns. There are those, for instance, of professional wives in professional jobs; or of working wives who have to go out to support the family. There are patterns with regard to the division of labour within the house and family. All these are matters which are changing and are important to the human institution of marriage. We are also becoming increasingly aware that the family and the parents in responsibility for the family cannot confine themselves to simply looking after their children, providing the best of educational and, indeed, of all possible worlds. We are becoming progressively aware that part of the parents' responsibility for the future of their children is their contribution to the kind of society in which their children will grow up. We are becoming progressively aware that we cannot opt out and say, 'I will look after my professional job and thereby earn enough to look after my children.' Because what is becoming even more important than the school I can afford to send my children to is the kind of society I tolerate and in which my children will develop and grow. So we must see marriage as moving out in this way, out of this relationship into concern for the community at large.

All this is some impression of the human institution we call marriage as we find it about us today. But that human institution has a Christian meaning. All human institutions now have some Christian meaning since the Word of God became flesh in Jesus Christ. All human institutions now that are of value are in some sense a bearer of this divine power. This is evident to us if we examine the message of the New Testament with regard to the central call to mankind which is to love of God and love of neighbour. And which then by St John in his first epistle and by St Paul in Corinthians and Galatians is in fact summed up simply in love of neighbour. It is above all in human relations that Christianity is realised, in our interaction with one another. It is here in meeting another person that the Incarnational fact is expressed for us, in the word we commonly use that salvation occurs; in some genuine living contact with another person that we benefit from the salvation which we consider to have been achieved for us in Christ. It is here we respond as brothers and sisters of one another. The gift has been given us through our incorporation into Christ in his sonship of the Father, so that we can never again see one another except in this way, and in so far as we treat one another in this way we realise in the world the sonship which was brought into the world by Jesus Christ and completed in his death and resurrection, and which is now our gift. So that in fact salvation takes place when we meet one another in a genuine human and loving way.

Marriage sees this particular powerful meeting of two people as a particular powerful bearer of this salvation. This has been brought out for us by St Paul's epistle to the Ephesians where he compares it, in continuity of course with the Old Testament, to the relationship between Christ and his Church and calls this whole reality he is talking about a great sacrament. Christ loved his people—his love for them, his contact with them, that is what saves them, what enables them to love in return and to love one another. And this is now shown forth and realised in every human contact or relationship. It is brought to our attention in a specific way according to St Paul in marriage, in that contact which enables two people to live together so that exchanging with one another at every level all of the time, they in fact embody the perfect example of how people should be in contact in love and therefore show forth Christ in the world.

It is the human reality in marriage which is the bearer of the divine. In thinking of marriage as a sacrament we may somehow get it the other way round. We may want to start from some religious ideas and we may forget that the religious ideas are embodied in the human reality. We may therefore overlook the human reality, we may neglect it and I am afraid we have neglected it. Therefore it would seem that the task which lies before us now, the task which we face as Christians involves reflecting more and more on our experience of the human reality and by reflecting on this to understand the Christian or divine meaning. One could take a number of examples of it. I have taken the one of salvation in this sense—that it is personal contact and the call which personal contact makes on us to respond that as it were brings us together, focuses us for the moment; where we were disintegrated beings we are faced with another person and called to understand, to respond and to love—we are brought together again. This is overcoming the division within us that we call sin, so that though we have found ourselves divided and dispersed, in this kind of human contact we can be unified in this way. This one aspect of how the human experience of relationship embodies the divine power in the world. And this of course is done over a continuous period and at a more profound level in marriage.

A second aspect of the task before us is that when we are

faced with somebody, brought into contact with somebody, and have to make a response, we make the response appropriate to the occasion while acknowledging that it is a response which can go on indefinitely, which may make further and indefinite demands on us, depending on the situation, on the opportunity for further relationship and so on. But some contacts will at certain stages in our lives make indefinite demands on us. In some contact we may be called in fact to make a sacrifice of ourselves, to give up ourselves. We may be called to follow Christ as he did in laying down his life. This may mean not literally but metaphorically, yet in a very painful way. It would seem indeed that all real human relationships mean moving out of oneself, abandoning oneself in order to understand and accept the other and then to be in turn reintegrated. And this is the death and resurrection, that he who will lose his life will find it, which recurs in the course of all our lives and this is what occurs particularly in marriage, when a person gives himself or herself away, and is received back in return. But marriage is also a disposing of oneself in a total way—which may seem all blissful and joyous at one moment but which in the course of life will surely come up against some very harsh realities that will show how far the self-giving we began with is now so fully rooted in us that we can follow through to the stage of accepting this aspect of marriage.

It is a limitation perhaps of our interpretation of marriage and Christian theology today, and indeed of our interpretation of life, that preoccupied as we are with the joy as it were of marriage and with the joyous aspects of life as manifest above all to us in the risen life of Christ, we may well forget that the only way to the Resurrection is through the Crucifixion, we may well forget that in giving ourselves away in any particular situation we have to be prepared to accept the painful consequence of dying to ourselves in this situation. This does not mean for a moment that we can tolerate suffering for others or in others if it is suffering which we can in any way remove; indeed the only justifiable giving of ourselves in this way which involves pain is in order to serve and love the others.

All this is part of our human experience which we can understand in the light of Christian revelation. Thus human experience understood in this way demands that in our attitude to marriage we reflect on the experience and so understand more fully the Christian meaning and dimension, how it embodies the divine in the world. But it demands more than understanding. It demands service. It demands that we be prepared as members of a community to do what we can in our own marriages and in our own lives, in our professional work and in our voluntary services, to enable the human institution of marriage to be realised as fully as possible in our society. Because unless we do that we are inhibiting the divine love in our society. Only through the medium of the human can that divine love come into our society. Therefore we must be serious in our own marriages in living and recognising the human dimension as much as possible. We must be serious in endeavouring to promote the services which are absolutely necessary in any society so that people can have a genuine human marriage: services in regard to health and education, and services in particular that take account of specific marital problems. There is no marriage without its problems because there are no human beings without problems. And if there were a marriage without problems it would I think be a dead marriage, a marriage not of this world, because it is the recurrence of these difficulties that challenges us to go out of ourselves. Not, let me repeat, that we can bear to stand by and see difficulties recur which we could remove. But people must be prepared for difficulties in marriage and see them as opportunities of growth. We all of us must also be prepared and willing to help organise the services that the problems which arise in marriage demand.

9

Ethical Problems of Abortion[1]

This chapter falls into three distinct sections. In the first I will resume briefly the position of the Roman Catholic Church and of the other Churches in their official statements and current theological opinion. It will help to set these positions in their historical and Christian context. The second section will seek to isolate the immediate key and controverted issues in this ethical and Christian tradition. The third and final section will consider some of the wider issues involved in discussing ethical problems of abortion. In this way it is hoped to set the discussion in its total framework.

I. THE CHRISTIAN POSITION ON ABORTION

Two reservations are in order here. I obviously cannot in the space available give a comprehensive account of all the positions held by Christians, past and present. In fact I will be mainly concerned with the position of my own Church, the Roman Catholic, as it is the one I know best. However, I consider it helpful to include here some account of non-Roman positions, at least, as further examples of how the common tradition has developed.

The second reservation concerns the propriety of considering abortion in Christian terms at all. It might seem that the title 'Ethical Problems of Abortion' suggests a non-religious approach, and that this would be the only profitable one in our post-Christian world. As a matter of history the Christian tradition provides the most considerable body of thought on the subject. As a way into the dicussion, which should not of course obscure ethical analysis by religious authority or sentiment, the Christian position is invaluable. Any particular statement of it may not be regarded as preventing further discussion but as a stimulus to it.

The Christian Churches Today

Roman Catholic Position. The present official position in the Roman Catholic Church was clearly and firmly laid down in the encyclical *Casti Connubii* of Pius XI in 1930,[2] reinforced by Pius XII in his Address to the Italian Catholic Society of Midwives, 1951[3] and confirmed by Vatican II, in its pastoral constitution, Joy and Hope, 1965.[4] In these documents the life of the fetus from the moment of conception is regarded as inviolable so that any direct attack on it as an end or a means is rejected as immoral. No medical, eugenic, social, ethical, or other indications are allowed as justifying 'direct' killing of what is recognised as an innocent human being from the moment of its conception. In the theological discussion which followed *Casti Connubii*, and which had preceded it, this 'hard line' was slightly modified by the acceptance of certain cases of 'indirect abortion', where the fetus was not regarded as the subject of direct attack. Its death, in the case of the removal of the cancerous womb and Fallopian tube with the ectopic pregnancy, was interpreted according to the principle of double effect as the regrettable, unavoidable, but indirect effect of an operation demanded by the woman's pathological condition.[5]

Other Christian Churches. In the other Christian Churches there has been a parallel concern for the protection of the life of the fetus. This has been combined with a greater readiness to admit exceptions for 'medical indications'. The report of the Committee on the Family in Contemporary Society at the Lambeth Conference of 1958 stated:

In the strongest terms, Christians reject the practice of induced abortion, or infanticide, which involves the killing of a life already conceived (as well as a violation of the personality of the mother), save at a time of strict and undeniable medical necessity. The plight of families, or indeed of governments trapped in hopeless poverty and overpopulation, may well help us understand why they think abortion more merciful than the slow starvation which looms ahead. Still, the sacredness of life is, in Christian eyes, an absolute which should not be violated.[6]

The Bishops' Encyclical Letter simply stated that in face of need for population control, 'Abortion and infanticide are to be condemned'.[7]

The American National Council of Churches through its General Board issued a rather less stringent statement on 23 February, 1961:

Protestant Christians are agreed in condemning abortions or any method which destroys human life except when the health or life of the mother is at stake. The destruction of human life already begun cannot be condoned as a method of family limitation. The ethical complexities involved in the practice of abortion related to abnormal circumstances need additional study by Christian scholars.[8]

The Evangelical Church in Germany presumed the justification of abortion for such reasons in 1963 when it took a stand against the justification of it for so-called 'ethical' reasons such as rape or incest.[9]

These positions have not remained static in the meantime and there is evidence of development both among the theologians and at a more official level. There is scarcely any Protestant theologian of repute who would now defend Dietrich Bonhoeffer's line in his *Ethics*:

Destruction of the embryo in the mother's womb is a violation of the right to live which God has bestowed upon this nascent life. To raise the question whether we are here concerned already with a human being or not is merely to confuse the issue. The simple fact is that God certainly intended to create a human being and that this nascent human being has been deliberately deprived of his life. And this is nothing but murder.[10]

In a footnote he approves the Roman Catholic position which excludes even danger to the life of the mother as a justifying cause. Here he would be entirely alone among his continental Protestant colleagues today.[11] Without presuming to give an exhaustive list, I find that the following known theologians all support medical indications for abortion: Karl Barth[12] and Alfred de Quervain[13] (Swiss), Dutchman Hendrik van Oyen,[14] Dane Nils Soe,[15] and the Germans Hans Fritzsche,[16] Helmut Thielecke[17], Wolfgang Trillhaas[18] and Karl Jansen.[19] Further indications are debated, with a tendency to extend life and health of the mother to include mental or psychiatric health and to a smaller degree social conditions. There is growing support also for 'eugenic indications' and 'ethical indications'.[20] All these extensions do not add up to a defence of abortion on demand and the sanctity of life in the womb is strongly insisted upon, although it may have to yield to 'higher values' in exceptional circumstances.

Amongst English-speaking Anglican and Protestant theologians agreement exists on medical indications. Apart from that there is considerable disagreement ranging from the very permissive attitude of Anglican Joseph Fletcher,[21] Professor at Union Seminary, New York ('No unwanted child should be born') to the very restrictive and closely argued position of Methodist Paul Ramsey,[22] Professor at Princeton University. The Church of England has produced a very considered and considerable study of the problem in recent times in a document published for the Church Assembly Board of Social Responsibility, entitled: *Abortion, An Ethical Discussion* (London 1965). Some of the points made will come up for discussion later. For the present it is sufficient to note that after careful discussion of the various indications and strongly affirming the general protection due to the fetus, it accepts that abortion can be justified where, with the necessary safeguards:

> it could be reasonably established that there was a threat to the mother's life or well-being, and hence inescapably to her health, if she were obliged to carry the child to term and give it birth. And our view is that, in reaching this conclusion, her life and well-being must be seen as integrally connected with the life and well-being of her family.[23]

Indications such as danger of abnormality in the child (eugenic) or pregnancy due to rape (ethical) are not regarded as justifying in themselves but only in so far as they involve 'a threat to the mother's life or well-being'. This could be interpreted as an extension of the previously accepted 'medical indications' but it does seem to go far beyond the Lambeth statement of 1958.

No comparable development exists in the Roman Church. The statement of Vatican II[24] and subsequent episcopal statements[25] in face of moves to liberalise civil laws on abortion have made no concession on the moral issue. Among the theologians there has been some sign of a reconsideration of medical indications, where the mother's life is in danger.[26] Little of this has yet appeared in print. As late as the end of the last century abortion to save the life of the mother was defended by reputable theologians.[27] A series of replies by the Holy Office (1884–1902) prepared the way for the definitive stand taken by Pius XI.[28] But, as we have seen, two exceptions have since received recognition by the theologians. To appreciate the main thrust of the Christian attitude to abortion and the place of exceptions, past and present, it is necessary to review (very briefly) the history of that attitude.

Historical Background[29]

Christianity was born into a world which accepted abortion in theory and practice. The Scriptures of the Old Testament, which provided so much for the doctrinal and moral enlightenment of the New Israel, did not offer any immediate guidance here. Yet as early as the end of the first century abortion was explicitly condemned. In this the Didache[30] was shortly followed by the Epistle of Barnabas[31] and so it goes on through Athenagoras,[32] Minucius Felix[33] and Tertullian[34] into the third century with Clement of Alexandria,[35] Cyprian,[36] through the fourth century Councils of Elvira[37] and Ancyra[38] to Jerome[39] and Augustine[40] in the West, Chrysostom[41] and Basil[42] of Cappadocia in the East.

In this formative period abortion was clearly condemned as violation of love of neighbour[43] and of the creative work of God.[44] It was usually classified with the serious sins forbidden by the Decalogue[45] and in the early stages equiparated to homicide.[46] Later distinction between formed, vivified and unformed fetus made no difference to its clearcut condemnation as wrong, if not as homicide.[47]

This condemnation was upheld in successive centuries.[48] It was incorporated in the penitentials,[49] confirmed in various councils and given lasting status in the collections of canon law begun by the Decree of Gratian.[50] The medieval theologians repeated the condemnation for any stage of the pregnancy, but only after ensoulment would Aquinas and others describe it as homicide,[51] and in this the canons agreed with them.[52] Theological analysis at this time revealed that not all killing could be regarded as wrong. Self-defence, war and punishment for crime were recognised as exceptions.[53] Not all the victims of these exceptions could be classified as guilty. However, the question of permitting abortion to save the life of the mother was not considered in this theological context, although the problem was mentioned in the medical texts of the time.[54]

The opinion of an obscure Dominican of Aquinas' time,

John of Naples,[55] favoured abortion to save the life of the
mother. This opinion was rescued and given currency by
St Antoninus of Florence[56] and later by Sylvester of Prieras,[57]
although neither adopted the opinion as his own. Thomas
Sanchez[58] (1550–1610), the great theologian of marriage
questions, did adopt it and offer an elaborate defence. In
the case of the unensouled fetus (up to 40 days), killing the
fetus was 'more probably' lawful, in order to save the life
of the mother, and similarly to save a girl whose relatives
would probably kill her if they discovered she was pregnant,
but not merely to protect a girl's reputation. Although
according to the medical biology of the time intercourse
just after conception carried high risk of abortion, it was
nevertheless allowed. For the ensouled fetus where the
mother's life was in danger and if the means did not tend
'directly' to kill the fetus, they could be used to save the
mother even though they carried a high risk of or were
equally directed to the killing of the fetus. Sanchez quotes
Aquinas on the lawfulness of killing another to save one's
own life but he does not provide a consequent and coherent
distinction of means. Where the means were equally direct
the mother's intention was decisive.

The Belgium Jesuit, Lessius[59] did not allow the direct
killing of the unensouled fetus, but his practical conclusions
were the same as he simply extended the principles applied
by Sanchez to the ensouled fetus to all stages of its development. Busenbaum,[60] a German Jesuit and one of the origina-
tors at the beginning of the seventeenth century of the moral
theology manual as we have known it, also defended abortion in these circumstances and in this he was followed by
the patron saint of moral theologians, St Alphonsus Liguori,[61]
in the middle of the eighteenth century. It was the predominant intention which counted but only some means
were allowed.

That the tendency of such otherwise influential moral
theologians to admit exceptions for abortion should have
been gradually discarded in the Roman Church was due to

a number of factors, already operative in the seventeenth and eighteenth centuries.[62] The first of these was authoritative decisions from Rome itself, which for reasons of prudence tended to extra protection to the fetus. The most interesting of these papal interventions was the condemnation by Innocent XI, in 1679, of 65 propositions taken from 100 submitted by theologians of Louvain as evidence of moral laxity. Propositions 34 and 35 concerned abortion:

> 34 It is lawful to procure abortion before ensoulment of the fetus, lest a girl, detected as pregnant, be killed or defamed.[63]
>
> 35 It seems probable that the fetus (as long as it is in the uterus) lacks a rational soul and begins first to have one when it is born; and consequently it must be said that no abortion is homicide.[64]

Although one of the cases defended by Sanchez as lawful was hereby condemned, the main theological position was untouched.

More important was the development of the view of the immediate or very early animation of the fetus by the rational soul.[65] A Louvain physician, Thomas Fienus, published a book in 1620 entitled: *A Book on the Formation of the Fetus in which it is shown that the Rational Soul is Infused on the Third Day*.[66] A year later a more influential work by the Roman physician Paul Zacchias appeared, rejecting the successive souls theory and maintaining that the rational soul must be infused at the first moment of conception.[67] The theologians, even more than 100 years later as in the case of Alphonsus, remained undisturbed by this. But the tendency was against the 'mediate' view. Another contributing factor was the growing devotion to the Immaculate Conception of Mary, which became a universal feast of obligation in 1701 and gave indirect support to the theory of 'immediate' animation.[68]

Theological reflection coupled with scientific discoveries

like that of the ovum (1827) finally installed the theory of immediate animation as almost universally accepted. The need to protect the fetus became more urgent also in the nineteenth century (and still more so in the twentieth), so that the Roman Church under the central direction of Rome returned to the earlier and harder line—before the moralists began to make their list of exceptions. The progress of this return through the Holy Office replies down to Vatican II we have already indicated.

In the historical development so briefly and crudely outlined here, and which, up to the sixteenth century at least, we share with Reformation Christians, the first global reaction in defence of the fetus as human and worthy of Christian love and protection, was modified more or less by different understanding on three points: the status of the fetus as ensouled and so fully human or no; the recognition that the commandment 'Thou shalt not kill' did not apply in some circumstances; the consideration of which values might permit departure from the commandment in particular circumstances. It is on their understanding of these three points that other Christians disagree with the official Roman position. A fresh consideration of them in the light of the historical background and of contemporary ethical thought, especially Christian, is demanded of Roman Catholics if they are to serve the Christian and Roman community as effectively as possible in the protection of nascent human life.

2. THE IMMEDIATE ISSUES

The Status of the Fetus

It is not for me to attempt any detailed biological discussion of the conceptus or fetus. I assume what seems to be agreed among biologists, that:

It is not an appendage or organ of the mother, but rather a separate organism; that it can be identified as belonging biologically to the human race; that it contains all of the genetic information that, during development, will interact with its environment to produce the complete human organism; that differences between the fetus shortly before birth and the infant shortly after birth are not biologically of basic significance; that no point in the development exists where the biological form and function of the body are suddenly added.[69]

In fact I assume that, as far as biology is concerned, what becomes our recognisable human being begins as a distinct organism with the conceptus, and that there is no further point where one can speak of such a radical discontinuity in development that it is possible for the biologist to be invoked as witness for the passage of the fetus from a sub-human to a human state at any particular time.

Theories of immediate or mediate animation cannot, it seems to me, expect now or perhaps ever any direct support from biology or the physical sciences. The arguments on either side are basically philosophical and theological. The older aristotelian and thomistic concept of 'a metamorphosis of souls' as the fetus went through successive vegetative, animal and human stages never entirely disappeared from theology. Cardinal Mercier defended it along with a small minority in this century.[70] The biological discoveries of the continuous development of the fetus from the fertilised ovum and the difficulties of conceiving such a succession of souls were considered very serious if not impossible difficulties.[71] The theory has, however, received some recent support in the abortion context through an article by the American Jesuit psychologist, Joseph Donceel,[72] and from others. Two main points are urged in its favour: the difficulty of understanding 'how the rational soul as the substantial form of a real human body can be present when the human body is not real but only virtually present in the cell or aggregate of cells';[73] the phenomenon of identical twins which result from the one ovum fertilised by a single spermatazoon, raising the difficulty of how if the human soul was present from the moment of fertilisation, it can now split into two souls.

Personally I do not see any way of settling this argument, between mediate and immediate animation. The soul-body analysis, for all the service it has given and still gives in other areas, may not be helpful here, at least as a starting point.

It is not easy to find a satisfactory alternative. In the Church of England study already cited the fetus is regarded as a potential human person. 'It is possible to argue that between the moment of conception and the full maturing of the personality—whenever that may be assumed to have been attained—there is a long period of development, and that the degree of protection which is this person's due develops *pari passu* with it.'[74] There are difficulties about this moral and juridical consequence, as it would seem to give those who need protection most, the undeveloped and weak, whether in or out of the womb, the least protection, in contradiction to what we normally regard as Christian and civilised. And potentially human applies to a man at every stage of his life—he is always on the way to realising his human potential.

The notion of the individual's potential humanity does involve another contemporary preoccupation about man, his historical condition. The complete human being exists in history. He has a history. He is a history. A description of John Smith on Saturday 11 May 1968, however exhaustive it may be and however much he may be regarded as having achieved maturity or even the climax of his life, is not complete. The complete description demands the future as well as the present and past. It must be extended from the first moment of his existence in history or in this world to his last.

His existence in history is a bodily existence. He is a history through his bodily presence to the cosmos and the human community. His bodily presence in the world may be distinguished by his capacity to take possession of himself and so of the relationships to the cosmos and the human community, without which he could not come into or continue in existence. His capacity to do this develops and is realised in history. If it is to develop and be realised, if the history of the individual member of the human race is to become human—that is, a realisation of his own capacity for self-possession and self-disposition in personal life and relationships—the human community must protect him especially in the early stages when he is incapable of protecting himself (and of course incapable of taking possession of himself).

This protection is obviously demanded after birth, but no less obviously before birth. Where the historical condition of man is taken in its full seriousness it is difficult to see why one stage of his existence should be entitled to less protection in principle than any other. All stages are equally essential to his human existence in history. In practice the weaker and less developed stages seem to have greater claim on the community and on those with whom he has, in his inchoative existence, the closest relationships. With this historical view of man the mediate-immediate animation debate might seem to be asking the wrong question, while the description of the fetus as merely potentially human is inadequate. Whatever the degree of its realised humanity, the fetus stage is an essential part of the whole man and so entitled to protection.

The Prohibitions of Homicide

Recognition of the fetus as an essential part of historical man and so entitled to protection from arbitrary destruction, does not immediately solve the moral problem of abortion. The questions must still be asked: How far does this protection extend for any human being—does the prohibition of human killing admit of any exceptions? Are there any features in fetal life or any peculiar circumstances which would suggest (or exclude) exceptions here?

The General Possibility of Exceptions. The Christian community has from the beginning adopted the formula of the fifth (sixth) commandment of the Decalogue as its own. Recent scholarship shows that this commandment not to kill, was in its original Israelite setting not comprehensive. The verb used, *rasach*, refers to 'illegal killing inimical in the community'.[75] It existed, however, in a community which had capital punishment, and in which war was permitted or even commanded. There is no evidence that it extended to abortion, which according to Exodus 21:22 seems to have been regarded rather as material damage, although in Assyrian law abortion was severely punished.[76] The Old Testament basis of the prohibition is indicated in Yahweh's words to Noah in Genesis 9:6: 'Whoever sheds the blood of man, by man shall his blood be shed; for God made man in his own image.' The revelation of Yahweh as lord of life and death underlines the limitations of human lordship over other men especially in matters of life and death.

In the New Testament the prohibition of homicide is taken for granted by Jesus and the apostolic writers. Jesus repeats it on a number of occasions,[77] only to extend it and deepen it. Not only may one not kill one's enemies but as a follower of Jesus one must love them (*Matt.* 5:21, 43–8). The central moral directive of the New Testament and the one to which all the others reduce, makes killing unthinkable (cf. *Mark* 12:28–34). The response of love to the neighbour demands respect for his actual existence as a necessary basis for the development and expression of this love. Man, who was made in the image of God and so sacred in his life, becomes through Christ a son of the father and brother of Christ and of his fellowmen (*Rom.* 13:8–10; *Gal.* 5:14). All murder is now fratricide. Despite this radical deepening of the Old Testament attitude there is no conclusive evidence that Jesus intended to rule out all the exceptions allowed there, although it would clearly be more difficult to justify them. The acceptance by Jesus of the state authority (cf. *Mark* 12:13–17) and its formal justification by Paul (*Rom.* 13:1–7) may imply the acceptance of exceptions like unavoidable war and capital punishment as social necessities of the time, but the weight of New Testament teaching is to make exceptions very difficult to justify.

Despite their consciousness of the new and radical character of the way of life prescribed for Christians as a way of love, the early Christian writers do not ignore their Old Testament inheritance. The commandments of the Decalogue are employed directly and indirectly in dealing with moral issues, in particular with the problem of life and death. But the very early Christian writers do have difficulties about accepting the pre-Christian exceptions of war and capital punishment and apply the deeper Christian understanding explicitly to rejection of abortion.[78] Their enthusiastic endorsement of martyrdom does, of course, reveal their awareness that human life could and in certain circumstances should be subordinated to higher values. It was, however, only after the Constantinian liberation (or captivity?) that Christian thinkers explicitly accepted war and capital punishment as compatible with Christian life and love.

In later theological reflection these exceptions were systematically defended, together with killing in self-defence. This has remained common theological teaching since among all Christians. Indeed it has become such a commonplace in Christian theory and practice that one must note Karl Barth's criticism of self-defence:

how far we have strayed from the command of God and obedience is to be revealed by the fact that what ought to be obvious and self-evident according to the command, namely the required renunciation of self-defence, has now become the normal and natural thing which we think we can do at once should the need arise.[79]

And, as he also points out, the highly exceptional circumstances which might justify capital punishment and war have long since been trivialised.[80] The awesome responsibility, which assuming power of life and death over another in such circumstances involves, has been emptied of much of its Christian meaning.

The prevailing Christian theological position, including Barth, does admit of exceptions to the prohibition of killing in exceptional cases. The justification of these has taken two forms, corresponding to two general types of situation.

In the first the Christian is considered to have forfeited his right to protection by his behaviour. So in the three usual exceptions—self-defence, just war and capital punishment—the assailant, the enemy soldier, the criminal, is no longer entitled to normal respect for his life and the individual/society may protect itself to the extent of destroying him, if necessary.

The second type of case is distinguished from the first by the fact that the victim has not forfeited his rights in any way and so may not be 'directly' killed but for the sake of some higher good his death is permitted or accepted as the inevitable result of the action performed to achieve some other good. The technical analysis of such an action has entered Catholic moral theology as the principle of double effect.[81]

At the 'macroscopic' level of human activity it has a definite validity. In the world in which we live every human action may have some evil effect. To live and act at all, it is necessary to accept, without willing or intending them, the unavoidable evil consequences of our (necessary) good actions. Two safeguards should be added to the invocation of the principle of double effect in matters of life and death, lest it become an easy escape from one's genuine responsibilities: is alternative action really impossible or just inconvenient and difficult for society as well as the individual? And how far are individual and social acts of *omission* which result in serious evil consequences (e.g. death) simply ignored or at least regarded as much less important than 'positive' actions?

The application of such a principle has been usual with Catholic theologians in justifying the killing of civilians

in war. Their deaths are not directly willed, but the unavoidable consequence of an act justified in itself, e.g.
the bombing of a military target. How hollow this kind of
justification has been in practice we have ample recent
evidence. The normal respect which human life should
evoke disappears in a mushroom cloud of smoke.

The key to the understanding and value of the principle
of double-effect lies in recognising that a good motive or
consequence is not sufficient to make a human act in its
totality good.[82] It cannot therefore, without violence to
moral analysis and discourse, be simply re-described in
terms of consequence or motive.[83] It is not enough to say of
Hiroshima that it shortened the war, or of Vietnam that it is
preventing the spread of Communism (supposing either of
these to be true). Certain actions are of such importance to
human welfare and ethics that they may not be elided into
their consequences or judged in terms of motive alone.
Actions involving the deaths of other human beings are such.

On this basis a distinction has been drawn between direct
and indirect killing. In the exceptional cases mentioned
above the killing has been for the most part treated as direct
and justified, as we have seen, on the basis of forfeiture of
right by the victim. In the case of civilians in war and
a host of other cases including that permitting the death of
the fetus as a result of treating the mother, the killing
has been described as indirect. Where the action was of its
'nature' directed to curing the mother, where the death of
the fetus was not independently willed and where there was
a higher or comparable good (the life of the mother) at
stake, the recent Catholic tradition accepts the lawfulness
of such treatment. Direct killing of the fetus as a means to
saving the mother has been rejected.

There is a great deal to be said for this position as an
analysis of the moral situation and as the only practical
coherent protection against an unlimited and unjustifiable
extension of abortion.

Certain difficulties have been raised against it in theory and in practice. At a certain level of analysis at any rate, it could be presented as a refusal to save one life out of two threatened. Again the development of medical techniques has made it more difficult to apply the direct/indirect distinction. Evidence of this is the acceptance by Catholic moralists of removal of a cancerous womb with non-viable fetus, and the still more tricky (morally speaking) removal of the ectopic pregnancy.[84] It requires considerable sophistication to distinguish these from some other non-acceptable (to Roman Catholic moralists) cases of therapeutic abortion.

Basis of Prohibition and of Exceptions. Here it is necessary to look again at the basis of the prohibition of killing. Human interdependence—of children and adults, of individuals and groups, and eventually of all men—is basic to all morality, secular and Christian. Their mutual rights and obligations originate from, maintain and are limited by these relationships of interdependence. It is the person in relationship or in community, not the isolated individual, who is the subject of rights and duties, who is a moral entity. The basic right of respect for the other's existence must not be separated from obligations to the quality of existence, but it does remain truly basic. And it is only in very exceptional cases that the Christian moral tradition allows anything to override that basic respect. The expression of respect for existence by refraining from injuring it, by protecting it and by serving the quality of it, varies according to the particular relationship and the capacity to protect and serve. People with a closer relationship have the more urgent obligation. People with greater resources have a more extensive one. In the Christian vision and modern technological unity one's responsibilities may extend to the ends of the earth.

Limitations of the obligation to protect and serve life are inevitable. They arise from the limited resources of individuals and groups, and the consequent need to make choices if the basic obligation is to be fulfilled at all. So protection and service of one individual or family or larger community involves limitation and choice with the exclusion (through inability) of service to some other individual or group. Such choice and exclusion can entail serious loss, even death, for the others if nobody else can or does attend to their needs.

The limitation of protection and service appears more acutely still, when the existence or action of one constitutes a 'positive' threat to the existence of others. Here Christian tradition and human ethical reflection recognise that respect for human life demands protection from attack, attack incompatible with a genuine human relationship. The initiator of the attack (the aggressor) must be restrained. The right and duty to restrain him do not depend on his formal guilt. (Some criminals are insane and most soldiers are in good faith.) The manner and extent of the restraint depend on what is necessary to incapacitate him in his aggression. The complications of modern war have shown how hard it is to distinguish defence from attack. The recent Arab-Israeli war is only one example, if a classic one, of the difficulties of making such a distinction. Where the defence or restraint must take the form of counter-attack in order to incapacitate the aggressor, the thrust of the action, as Paul Ramsey[85] has recently emphasised, is the incapacitation of assailant (criminal or soldier) not his death. So one does not shoot prisoners of war and it is difficult to see how capital punishment is justified in the modern developed state. The tradition does reasonably recognise the right of defence even unto the death of the other, if the aggression cannot be restrained short of that.

This moral understanding has been traditionally explained in terms of the distinction between direct and indirect killing. The absolute prohibition of direct killing of the innocent maintained in summary that the respect due to the life of the other was such that it was never at one's disposal. On the other hand the acceptance of killing of the unjust aggressor in some circumstances or the indirect killing of the innocent in others was demanded by the need to make certain choices in conflict situations. It may be asked if the distinction is the most effective way of preserving the undoubted truth in this traditional analysis. In one important way it is too 'lax', suggesting that the death of the enemy is the proper object of one's action, and not the stopping of the aggression. (The preoccupation with the number of enemy killed in the Vietnam war is a horrible reminder of how our thinking may develop.) In the same way it takes capital punishment much too lightly. In another way it provides rather inadequate criteria for distinguishing just and unjust aggression and for the distinction between direct and indirect killing in some of the difficult cases posed by modern obstetrics. The ectopic pregnancy offers an obvious example. As a summary and guideline it retains its importance for most cases, but if it is to be properly understood and used it needs to be set in the context of human relationships from which it has been abstracted.

The Mother-Fetus Relationship. Applying all this to the peculiar relationship of mother and fetus is no easy task. There is no relationship quite so intimate as that of mother and unborn child, no responsibility quite so immediate. The psychological dimension of the relationship may be totally unformed on one side and very unspecified on the other, yet the physical dependence and relationship is at its greatest. The responsibilities of the mother are correspondingly great. All the care which she must take relates to the fact that nobody else at this stage can assume any of her responsibility.

The first consequence of the peculiar mother-fetus relationship would suggest that more is demanded of the mother than in any other relationship between humans. And this clearly involves more self-sacrifice, an inescapable part of all relationship. The very reluctant exceptions allowed in regard to respect for life, may expect further limitations here.

There are other aspects. The very intimacy of the physical relationship allows the fetus to constitute a threat to the mother's life (and vice versa) in a way inconceivable in any other relationship. The phenomenon is *sui generis*. Again cases are alleged to arise where if no abortion takes place both mother and fetus will die, and for which we have no very helpful analogy. Finally the peculiarity of the mother's relationship with the fetus does not eliminate her relationships with and responsibility for other members of the family.

The question which must now be asked is whether the obligation to protect and serve the life of the fetus may not cease in certain circumstances and what these circumstances may be. It is accepted in the cases of indirect abortion that respect due to the life of the fetus may cease in case of danger to the life of the mother and where the saving of her life does not involve 'direct killing' of the fetus. Not all Christian moralists accept this and various attempts are made to provide alternative analyses while preserving the basic respect for life.

One of the most important of these has been given by Paul Ramsey,[86] whose thought is very much in the Catholic tradition of morality. He describes the situation of threat to the life of the mother as one of 'material' aggression by the fetus. And it is, he maintains, not unjust but material aggression which in the traditional teaching has justified intervention not to kill the material agressor, but to incapacitate him in his aggression. Such intervention to abort in case of danger of death to the mother would also be justified. This analysis has a certain attraction, as the Jesuit moral theologian Richard McCormack admits.[87]

Because of the very peculiar relationship of mother and fetus it is very difficult to draw exact analogies with the relationship between two separate people. The description then of the fetus in the womb behaving exactly as it should (and ignoring the rather ambiguous adjective 'innocent'), in terms of any kind of aggression (however technical and material), does not seem to offer a finally satisfactory basis for dealing with this problem.

In our analysis of human actions, the consequence or motive, we have said, may not simply be substituted for a description of the moral act. Yet in some circumstances the temporal and physical elements of the act may not constitute a moral unity until they are brought under the polarising influence of some consciously sought motive or consequence, or rather they may constitute different moral actions according to their different motives/consequences. For this the elements themselves must be capable of different immediate interpretations and the consequence or motive must be closely related to these, so closely as to provide the obvious polarising force. Thus removing an organ from the body may be an act of mutilation and so immoral, or a necessary operation (even though the organ itself is not diseased), or an act of self-sacrifice in the case of transplantation and so moral.

The fetus is not an organ of the mother's body, and so the example given must not be substituted for the analysis itself. But neither is the fetus separate or (*ex hypothesi*) separable from the mother, so the examples involving separate human beings which would see the death of one as already polarising the action (as a means to the good motive or consequence) may not be invoked too easily either. In the special situation, perhaps, the medical intervention receives its primary and prevailing polarisation from the motive—to save the mother's life. The general conclusion was supported in earlier Catholic theology to some extent. It is a common position among Protestants today and has been suggested by at least one recent Catholic writer.[88] The supporting analysis has not been invoked but some such seems necessary. The analysis itself does not seem entirely convincing although it might make more sense of the ectopic pregnancy case. It is perhaps too concerned with individual actions and too little with the relationships involved, and in a way from which moral analysis has suffered too much in the past.

A rather different analysis might consider precisely the web of relationships in which mother and fetus exist. The protection and service which the mother-in-community (of family and wider community with its social and medical services etc.) owes the fetus is special but not unlimited, any more than in other relationships. Catholic moralists accept, as we know, that it ceases in cases of indirect abortion. Can it cease in other situations where the life of the mother (or both) is immediately threatened so that her obligations to her family (and herself) and their rights prevail? Can the direct physical intervention in that case be interpreted morally as simply taking account of the rights which prevail? Has the fetus, in the hard choices which have to be made, to yield its claim, in the sense that the choice-makers may opt to save the life of the mother even by the direct removal of a non-viable fetus? Does the traditional understanding then of the distinction between direct and indirect abortion lean too heavily on physical criteria that no longer apply? These are not easy questions to answer but in searching for answers one may arrive at a more correct and refined analysis of the abortion problem than has yet appeared without yielding on the central commitment to the protection of human life at all stages.

In the face of all possible extension of the present exceptions two questions remain: would any justification of the hard case (danger of death) lead logically, theologically or sociologically to the acceptance of unlimited and unjustifiable abortion? how does the Christian faith with its deep sense of self-sacrifice in service of the other affect the personal decision to be made? We will turn our attention now to these two questions.

The Indications for Abortion

In all this discussion I have had a depressing feeling of irrelevance, because of two question marks in my mind. How far are there genuine cases of danger to the mother's life any more? Even if there are, is not the current concern with abortion something much wider, in which the debate about saving the life of the mother is only of value as a lead into discussing all the other possible indications?[89] To ensure some contact with reality I now turn to these other indications.

The 'Medical' Indications. The medical indications for abortion have proved in the theological discussion the predominant but not the only ones. In recent times these indications have been extended by most defenders of abortion for medical reasons to include what the Church of England study calls 'the psycho-physical well-being of the mother'.[90] Not merely the mother's continued historical existence, but the quality of that existence is hereby invoked as justifying the termination of the existence of the fetus. This was the extension suggested by Judge Macnaghten in his direction to the jury in the celebrated 'Bourne case' in England in 1937.[91] The reluctance of moral theologians to make this extension is, according to the Church of England pamphlet, to be explained by their fears of further (and indefinite) extension.[92] In this their fears may well have proved to be justified. However, some examination of the extension in itself may help.

It must be stressed, above all to and by Roman Catholics, that our obligations to the other are not to be thought of primarily and exclusively in terms of his actual existence, but rather in terms of the quality of that existence. Our obligation as human beings and Christians is to recognise, protect, serve and love our neighbour in his concrete existence, not just to allow him to exist. In Christian shorthand it is to love our neighbour. This demands, primarily, positive action from us in accordance with our capacities, which include the closeness, by origin or development, of our relation with this person as well as our spiritual, psychic and physical resources. It is only in the extreme case where our other more urgent obligations do not allow us to give the necessary help that we may neglect the quality and, in still more extreme cases, the actuality of this existence. To suppress this existence in more positive fashion is a further step again. (But this we have already seen.) So even if one could justify abortion in the case of conflict between two actual existences, to do so to enhance the quality of one is clearly more difficult, and it might introduce an exception to the prohibition of

homicide that is so far beyond the traditional ones as to be
new in kind. It is hard to see the right to existence of the
fetus ceasing in face of the *quality* of existence of the mother,
for instance, or how it could be described in terms of material
aggression. Yet it remains true that actual existence is not
the term of the doctor's or the community's responsibility
where the mother is concerned. There remains the factual
question of alternative means of serving this quality. But
here it may help to consider the other indications.

Psychological Indications. The extension of medical indications for any intervention so as to include psychological ones
would be normal enough. There might be at least one more
compelling reason for doing so in the situation where there
was a real danger of suicide in a patient whose depression
was due to the pregnancy and could only be treated by
removing the cause. Again one wonders about the actuality
of these cases and the possibility of alternative treatments.
As against the analysis of physical threat to life, it is more
difficult to see the fetus constituting, in Paul Ramsey's
terms, a material aggression; it is also difficult to see the
abortion yielding to description in terms of saving the
mother's life as its primary thrust, or to see the fetus as
having to yield its right to existence in the context of the
relationship.

Socio-Economic Indications. Many people, including the
legislators in Britain, Colorado and California last year,[93]
and some Christian theologians, have already moved from
medical, including psychological, indications to accepting
the social and economic conditions of the mother as justifying abortion. And this step may be taken for at least two
good reasons.

The mother is not a physical reality merely, not even a
psycho-physical reality but a socio-psycho-physical reality.
She exists as a person only in community or society. The
quality of her existence depends not simply on her physical
or psychic well-being. These cannot, in fact, be isolated
from her social well-being. And our obligations to her are

to this socio-psycho-somatic entity. It is a further hard fact that her total well-being in this sense is related to her economic circumstances. The second good reason recognises the appalling social and economic circumstances in which so many people live today, wishes to spare families in these conditions the burden of further children, and to give the society in which they live a chance, through population control, to develop economically and socially. A further reason—to save the child such a miserable existence—is best considered separately with eugenic indications.

Again the argument turns on the quality of existence for the mother, the already existing family and wider society perhaps. Abortion is being used as a form of family planning, where other means have been used and failed or where no such means have been or could be used. One's first reaction is to call for greater education in more acceptable family planning measures and more widespread use of these, although this may exacerbate a particular case, when such measures fail. At any rate, once the pregnancy is there, it has to be considered whether abortion could be justified.

There can be no doubting certain facts here: that such cases of severe socio-economic hardship exist, and that for the foreseeable future family planning methods will not eliminate them entirely. But can the suppression of human existence at the inchoative stage be justified for what it will add to the quality of the life of the mother, family or society? Will the narrow restrictions imposed on exceptions to the prohibition of taking human life suddenly appear juvenile and irrelevant in face of the justification of such a vast and indeterminate number of abortions? And what does this involve for the quality of our society?

Eugenic Indications. Here we are concerned with the quality of existence which the fetus can hope to enjoy after birth, in particular the probability of deficiency or deformity as a justification for abortion. In the classic expression of the case, the abortion is performed not for the sake of the

mother but for the sake of the child.[94] (The influence of
the deficient children on the future race—the genetic pool—
should be considered under social indications.) It would
be unfair to summarise it as seeking to serve the quality of
the child's existence by eliminating that existence. But it
does involve a judgement by a second party, as to what
quality of existence is acceptable to another, judging that
quality on the basis of the fairly crude standards of physical
or mental capacity and arriving at that judgement in a
situation fraught with uncertainties. Would the granting of
such power to another at the beginning (or end) of life alter
our Christian and western concept of man in his integrity
in a radical way? Substituting the social deficiency of the
previous category as justifying killing the fetus for his own
sake, would constitute the same moral problem.

The Anglican study group rejects this indication in itself,
but allows that the prospect of such a deformed child might
so affect the mother's health, or its arrival place such a
strain on her or on the family that the abortion could be
justified on the basis of the mother's well-being taken in the
context of her family.[95]

Ethical Indications. One of the most discussed problems in
recent German writing on the subject is the justification of
abortion after rape or other sexual offence.[96] The pain
involved for the prospective mother in such cases does not
call for any sentimentalising here. The obligations of the
community to these mothers can hardly be overstressed. But
the hard choice remains. Can the suppression of the existing
fetus be justified for the sake of the quality of existence of the
mother? Does the fact that this pregnancy originated in an
act of violence rather than in an act of love give the mother
rights over it which she would not otherwise have? Can the
fetus not be regarded as a gift of God in these circumstances?
Is there no way of serving and enhancing the quality of the
mother's existence without resorting to abortion? Presum-
ably the answers to these questions will vary with the situation but also according to one's prior attitude to the human-

ity or no of the fetus and with the extent to which one takes seriously the inviolability of human life.

This brief survey of the usual indications does scant justice to the personal suffering they frequently involve for the mothers and families in question. Each has so many unique features that little good would be achieved by rehearsing the more common features here. The omission should not be construed as though I thought that they were unimportant, even as far as moral decision is concerned. Far from that, they spell out very clearly the moral challenge which each case presents to neighbour and community. They define the demands which mother, child and family have on all of us in seeking to protect and cherish human beings entrusted to our care, and suggest that we may not scamp our obligations by simply calling for the suppression of the inconvenient existence in any given case, or by simply proclaiming strongly the immorality of abortion.

3 THE WIDER ISSUES

So far I have confined discussion pretty rigidly to narrowly ethical issues involved. The Christian tradition has been invoked mainly as a historical source of reflection on these issues. Yet the argument tended always to break out of these limitations into the wider issues of the nature and validity of moral argument, the relevance of a Christian point of view and the relation of this problem to the shape of human society. I would like to conclude by some brief consideration of these wider issues.

Moral Argument

The process whereby we acquire and change our moral attitudes is long and complex. For my purposes it will be useful to distinguish four elements in that process: that of external tradition or authority; personal reflection or intuition; experiences of one's own or of others; one's basic stance or attitude to the world.

Many or all of our moral attitudes may come under more than one, even all of these elements and the fourth is mainly of importance because of the way it affects the other three. It is necessary to consider each in turn and see its relevance for the problem.

External Tradition or Authority. It is from such an external tradition or authority that each man receives his first moral attitudes. This will normally be from his parents, but in the context of the society in which they live. School and/or religion quickly become distinct sources. Yet it should be clear that this tradition is not handed on merely in verbal form, oral or written, but is embodied in the structures which the becoming person encounters in society (e.g. racial discrimination), in the unspoken attitudes of the people who influence him and in the behaviour of those about him. The tradition is not necessarily religious. The external authority which influences a man in forming, retaining or changing his moral judgements varies with his circumstances from parent, teacher, bishop or other religious leader to a novelist like Camus, a philosopher like Marx, a revolutionary like Che Guevara, a famous film star, TV personality, or even one's barber. What is common here is the acceptance of one's moral views from others not on the basis of one's personal analysis but on the basis of the position of authority consciously or unconsciously accorded to this person or class of persons (bishops, scientists). 'They understand these affairs and one can safely rely on them.'

This is not a plea for the simple acceptance or rejection in moral issues of authoritative statements by so-called moral leaders. *Au contraire* I believe a man has an obligation to seek for that personal understanding which I shall discuss as the second element. Here I wish to emphasise that the new authoritarianism in morals may come from secular sources and if it lacks the rigidity of its religious predecessor it may have some of the capriciousness of fashion. There is a danger in a fundamental debate about life or death questions that the conclusions of scientists or what modern men think may be given undue importance, until the conclusions can be objectively evaluated and the thoughts fully reflected on. The fact that many people today find it difficult to regard the fetus in its early stages as human must be taken into account, but not automatically invested with unshakeable authority. That some women have no guilt feelings after abortion is another interesting fact but capable of many interpretations.

Personal Reflection. Without a moral tradition the individual could not make a start in moral activity or thought. But this tradition is not to be passively received. It must become, at least in its central affirmations and those which touch the recipient most nearly, the object of his reflection. Only in this way does it become his personal possession and a worthy instrument to help him in guiding his life.

In the course of such reflection (and it is a life task), he will grasp certain values as good, and the denial of them as bad. These may be very few and very indeterminate but this kind of understanding of truthfulness or generosity or courage or love as good and to be cherished is at least very widespread and for most of us forms an important part of our moral attitudes.

The values personally apprehended in reflection are not, at this level, either acts or rules about acts. The reflection may go further, so that one sees that certain acts or rules are necessary or appropriate expressions of these values. So when on reflection we grasp the notion of respect for the other, we do not immediately translate this into a rule that we may never kill him, still less do we see the possibility of exceptions to such a rule. For this further stage we need to consider fuller human experience, either personal or by proxy.

The Role of Experience. Normal experience demands that we translate our values into actions and if life can be granted the continuity it seems to demand, into some kinds of rules of action. Here a notable difference emerges in the way values yield to rules. The value is something which we have recognised as good and therefore to be preserved and fostered. But there seems in experience to be a very large number of ways in which this can be done. Therefore our positive rules of action, of what is to be done, seem rather indefinite. This is a sign of the creative richness of the value, but it can appear unhelpful to the immature who need more definite guidance. On the other hand it may be much easier to pinpoint what destroys or opposes a certain value. So our rules of prohibition, derived from values, are much more definite. This is a help in a negative way as it prevents one from following false paths in seeking to realise the value. However, the very definiteness of the negative rule gives it a certain fascination for supporter and opponent, so that the debate about a particular moral value is carried on at a secondary level in terms of rule and in terms of the rule most removed from the value in question, that which defines its negative limit.

The rules which we form, then, are an attempt in the light of experience to maintain and develop a certain value. In the case of respect for the historical existence and integrity of another human being, we are at the bedrock of human values. The respect is a very positive demand on us, involving caring for his needs at all the various levels of his existence. Because these are so various and can be fulfilled in so many different ways by so many people, it is not easy to formulate brief, clear and definite rules for the realisation of this respect.

One obvious general rule is that one is bound to render some essential service to another, where nobody else can render it. And an obvious example of that would be the care which a pregnant woman owes to the child in her womb. One could and should go on giving examples of general rules of positive action demanded in the service of life, because undoubtedly failure to uphold and realise this value occurs much more by omission, failure to take positive action, than by commission, performance of some action opposed to the value.

Again the negative rules are more definite and clear: Thou

shalt not kill. This rule reflects the basic opposition to the realisation of the value which killing involves. It has a very important negative role but it is no substitute for the understanding and realisation of the value. It describes a class of action through which the value cannot be realised, and is in fact destroyed. It offers little help in understanding or realising the value otherwise. Even as a negative rule it is approximate, and has to be refined in the light of experience.

The relevance of all this would seem to me to be that the debate about abortion should not be carried on primarily in terms of a rule, a negative rule and exceptions to it, if justice is to be done to the issues at stake, but rather in terms of the response demanded of individuals and society to the particular human need. It would be a frightful comment on our society if the central mother-child relationship were formulated in terms of 'you may not kill it except . . . or permit its death except. . . .'

Basic Attitude to the World. In the discussion of moral argument and values there remains the very large X-factor of a man's basic attitude to the world. How he eventually reacts to moral traditions and authorities will be greatly influenced by this world-view. Somebody with a Christian world-view may be expected to give great weight to the biblical teaching, to Christian tradition, etc. A secularist will react quite differently to the same authorities but will have his own 'sacred' books and authorities. Personal reflection will also be affected to the extent that his world-view has permeated his thinking. And so with the lessons of experience, personal and vicarious.

Lest this seem to exclude all possibility of dialogue on moral issues between people with diverging world-views, I hasten to add a number of clarifications. World-views are not necessarily and totally exclusive of one another. Today we are discovering convergences in the most unlikely places. They do not affect all moral understanding to the same degree. And, of course, actual people are more or less influenced by what they would consider their prevailing world-view. Still it remains a seriously complicating factor in any intricate moral debate. The debate on abortion is an excellent example. To illustrate that I move on to the wider issue next in line, the Christian perspective.

The Christian Perspective

For the Christian, the tradition, the values and the rules are not a group of disembodied abstractions, however admirable. They are given flesh and blood in the person of Jesus Christ, in which our understanding of man and his dignity is finally grounded. That meaning and that dignity reveals man as sharing the otherness (holiness) of God by being called to share in sonship of the Father, in brotherhood of Jesus and of one another. The Christian recognises that each man enjoys this call, that his attainment of it spells his personal perfection or maturity and that he can answer the call only in this world, in history and in community. It is a cosmic and community end to which he is called and it is in a cosmic and community way that he must answer it.

The response is the response of sonship and brotherhood through love of God and of the neighbour. The traditions, in so far as they are genuinely Christian and not corrupted by the selfishness of man as they frequently are, will introduce him to this good news. They will present him with a vision for man which did not originate with man and cannot be realised by man on his own. This is the vision of a developing community of mankind in which through their mutual relations men express their common sonship of God and brotherhood of one another. The values which they cherish as moral are partial but essential expressions of the personal perfection-in-community to which they are called. It is their basis in the inviolable dignity of man called to be son of God that makes these values valuable ultimately. The moral activity of the Christian is not the realisation of some abstract value, still less obedience to some abstract rule. It is a personal response to other persons, to whom he is bound by ties deeper than any human blood. It is in the love and service of persons that his moral life is realised. But the persons may not be confined to his own immediate friends or acquaintances. His neighbour is all mankind, and not as a series of isolated individuals, but as existing in a community which knows no division between Jew and Gentile, bond and free. It is to the personal service of others that the Christian sees his call. And this service takes the two related forms of direct service to the individual and service to the community within which the individual must exist, develop and make his own response.

It is not possible to separate person and community. One is not intelligible or realistic without the other. Each of us is committed to the service of both or rather of the one reality of persons-in-community or community of persons. And our commitment may be further specified as the building of that community of all mankind to which men are summoned in Christ.

The individual person (-in-community) forms a centre or nucleus within that community, whose uniqueness and inviolability is fully revealed in the Christian perspective. It is faced with this other, now known to share the very otherness of God, that the indefinite extent of his claim on one emerges in all its crucial outlines; that the horror of suppressing him for one's own convenience appears in all its starkness. The positive and negative aspects of respect for life acquire a new dimension in the Christian perspective.

The Christian message is primarily a positive message about man, his salvation or perfection by sharing this sonship and brotherhood, by entering into the building of the total human community. Here the quality of life or existence is given its full value. And the service of that quality in the other becomes the distinguishing feature of professed Christians.

Faced with a problem such as abortion it is un-Christian merely to say simply: Thou shalt not. This is not where the response to neighbour ought to begin and not where the debate ought to begin. The first Christian reaction must be to examine what can be done for neighbours in need, mothers and children. This must be given effective expression at the social level in dealing with the general problem, and at individual level in dealing with the particular problem. Anybody who does not take these primary obligations seriously has no right to cry halt, in the name of Christ. The deeper understanding that Christianity gives is that two-edged sword of the gospel, which may be easily used to cut the ground from under one's own feet. In this connection it is encouraging to read in the statement of the Canadian bishops the stress they lay on positive action to reduce the causes for abortion. Now if one of them were to take an unwed mother with this problem into his household! Words of a positive kind are better than mere negatives but the language these people will understand is loving action, the language of Christ.

In presenting the necessary prohibitions which respect for life as an expression of love of neighbour implies, a sense of proportion is very necessary in regard to both the extent of the evil and the circumstances of those responsible. So war, which must be presumed to be wrong until the contrary is clear, certain methods in war like indiscriminate bombing or use of napalm, capital punishment, the defence of certain class and property interests which are destroying other people no less surely if more slowly than the gas-chamber— all these merit clear condemnation as more extensive in their destruction of life and often without the extenuating circumstances that sometimes drive hapless mothers to abortion. It is a measure of the narrow individualism of our ethical thinking that such individual failures are more clearly and consistently attacked than social ones.

The role of the Christian Church here as elsewhere is to offer a lead in analysing and tackling the problem in a positive fashion, in the interests of humanising the world, of building a fuller human community, of ensuring for each individual the highest possible quality of life. With its understanding and resources it can and must help mankind to avoid any convenient short-term solutions, which ultimately tend to dehumanise the world and society. Its role as witness will be effective only in so far as its words describe the positive and primary call, as the negative limits are presented in correct proportions and as positive action at the individual and social level shows that the words mean something.

10

The Declaration on Religious Freedom

THE Declaration on Religious Liberty issued by the Second Vatican Council was debated and accepted in an atmosphere of recurring crisis. The original document was revised seven times. From its first introduction at the second session in November 1963 to its promulgation at the fourth and last in December 1965, it enjoyed the most enthusiastic support and the bitterest opposition. The opposition was relatively small—about 250 fathers—but it was persistent and highly organised. It prevented any vote on the proposed document until the last session and the postponement of a vote at the end of the third session led to the dramatic collection in St Peter's of almost 500 signatures to a protest document which was taken directly to the Pope by Cardinals Meyer, Leger and Ritter. Despite the revisions—including the introduction of some reassuring passages about the reality of the one true religion revealed by God in Christ and now 'subsisting' in the Roman Catholic Church—the opposition was maintained even in the last vote (249 negative votes 19 November 1965). Only at the formal final vote in the public assembly of 7 December 1965 did the negative votes fall to seventy.

This opposition was in fact a reflection of the consistency on both sides, for and against the Declaration. It stimulated the necessary hardheaded reflection by the upholders of the Declaration. And in spite of some irrelevancies and ambiguities, the Declaration emerged as a generally satisfactory statement of religious freedom as that term has been technically understood in recent years. The Declaration is limited in its scope and there is no point in criticising it for not doing things it was never intended to do. My task here is to outline the meaning and value of the Declaration and then to set it in the context of Vatican II, in relation to the other Constitutions, Decrees and Declarations.

The Title and Introduction

The title 'A Declaration on Religious Freedom: on the right of the person and communities to social and civil freedom in matters religious', indicates the intention and approach. The intention is to deal with the religious activities of individual persons and communities and the freedom they enjoy in society and especially in civil society as organised by the state. It is a *social* freedom then in relation to other men and to society that is in question.

And it is *freedom*. By its use of this word the Declaration reveals its approach as differing from that of some Catholic spokesmen and authors in the recent past who would allow *freedom* for the one true religion and only *tolerance* in society for all others. The Declaration never speaks of tolerance and its intention and argumentation make it clear that the freedom applies equally to men of all religions and none. Otherwise it could not in the modern context use this term religious freedom.

The early part of the Declaration explains the meaning of this freedom, gives its basis and outlines its range and limits. It defines the freedom in question as man's immunity from coercion by other men in seeking, professing, living and propagating that truth about himself and his destiny which we call religion (art. 2). And this applies both to man as an individual and to man acting in community or socially. At the very beginning, however, lest there should be any possible doubt and in an attempt to convert the minority (vainly as it turned out), the Declaration acknowledges the existence of the one true religion revealed by God in Christ and now 'subsisting' in the 'Catholic and apostolic Church' which all men are ultimately and objectively bound to accept (art. 1). The right to religious freedom as proposed by the Vatican Council in no way implies relativism or indifferentism in religion, that one religion is as good or as bad, as true or as false as another, or that it does not matter what religion a man has. Man is obliged before God to seek the truth revealed by God and to live according to it. The right of *'the person to social and civil freedom in matters religious'* in no way diminishes that obligation. In fact, as we shall see and as Bishop Ancel so forcibly pointed out in the Council debate, the obligation to the truth and the right to freedom necessarily complement each other.

The Meaning of the Right

Article 2 opens with an unambiguous declaration of the right to religious freedom: 'This Vatican Council declares that the human person has the right to religious freedom.' And the freedom means 'immunity from coercion on the part of individuals or of social groups and of any human power' in regard to religious matters. It is a right to immunity from coercion by other human beings in regard to his religious beliefs and practices—not any right against God to ignore or reject the truth revealed by him. As the lawful and actual possessor of the power of coercion, the state is especially concerned with this right and should so recognise and respect it that it becomes a 'civil right' (art. 2). The range as well as the limits of the right will be more properly appreciated when its basis has been examined. Meanwhile it is worth noting that this article gives the clearest and most forthright statement of religious liberty ever made in an official Church document, going beyond the welcome statement of Pope John in *Pacem in Terris*: 'Every human being has the right to honour God according to the sincere dictates of conscience (ad rectam conscientiae suae normam) and therefore the right to worship God privately and publicly.' The immunity from coercion recognised by the

Declaration is universal. It applies to all men, sincere and insincere. And it demands recognition as a civil right.

The Basis of Right

It is by its understanding of the basis of the right that Vatican II is able to make such a real advance. The previous debate had frequently got bogged down in statements like 'Error has no rights'. Only persons have rights, not abstractions like truth or error. Similarly any argument of the type: 'Persons in error may not have equal rights with those in truth', clouds the issue. Persons have rights in relation to other persons and in relation to the organisation of other persons in society. The right to religious freedom is a right in relation to other persons and to society. And it is a right to immunity from coercion in religious matters which arises from the truth, objective truth, of man's personal worth and dignity. As a knowing free being he seeks the truth about himself and his destiny. He lives that truth freely as he sees it. This is his distinguishing feature as a human being, as a person. No other human beings individually or collectively may remove this from him without destroying his value and worth as a person. The society which does this is no longer a human society of human beings for human beings.

This understanding of the basis of religious freedom avoids all the confusions of the rights of error, even of the rights of the 'sincere conscience' approach. It is impossible and unnecessary to distinguish the sincere from the insincere as far as the recognition of immunity is concerned. The right is not to profess or propagate error but to an immunity from coercion which is objectively good and founded in the objective truth of man's personal dignity and worth as a knowing, free being (art. 2).

In a world which is becoming technically one and so must ultimately find some political unity, this argument has a certain universal appeal. For Christian and non-Christian, theist and atheist, man is accepted in practice as a knowing,

free being. So there is a real possibility of practical agreement on the meaning and basis of religious freedom.

For theists and Christians man's capacity to know and
choose freely derives from his being created in the image of
God. In the divine plan man must in accordance with these
God-given abilities seek the truth about himself in freedom.
Social coercion would disrupt this divine plan for mankind
which is realised fully in Christ. In a later section (art. 9f.)
the Declaration shows how this notion of religious freedom
has its roots in revelation.

God's approach to mankind as summed up in Christ is an
invitation freely issued out of love, calling for man's free and
loving response. As the initiation of this response, 'the act
of faith is of its very nature a free act' (art. 10). This has
been a constant of the Church's teaching from the beginning.
As the unfashionable Code of Canon Law puts it: *Nemo
cogatur ad amplexandam fidem Catholicam.* Nobody may be
compelled to embrace the Catholic faith (Can. 1351). A
coerced faith or religious worship is of no value to the God
worshipped, as the Christian writer Tertullian wrote to the
Roman proconsul in Africa at the beginning of the third
century. The God of Christianity wants men's hearts, not
their external actions, even sacrifices. And coercion is not
the way to man's heart. Despite various deviations and
obscurities, the Church has always clung to this freedom of
the act of faith. Its full implications have been realised only
partially and gradually. Today immunity from any social
coercion is finally and fully understood as a necessary
implication of the freedom of the act of faith.

The personal attitude and activity of Christ, which for
Christians constitutes the pattern of their attitude and
activity, reveals more clearly still the necessity for such
social freedom (art. 11). His way of bearing witness to the
truth, of presenting the way of salvation as a message of love
from his Father for mankind, of patiently proposing but
never imposing the truth, provided a headline which was
followed by the apostolic Church which he founded. It is

in the preaching of Christ and the apostles that the Declaration urges us to find the model for all missionary activity, which may never resort to the unfair means of social coercion. In turn the Christian Church has a right to freedom in preaching its message, a right based on its God-given mission but effectively guaranteed in the general recognition of religious freedom as proposed in the Declaration (art. 13). At an earlier stage in the Church-state argument it is pointed out that man's essential relations with God are superior to the temporal order which is the concern of civil society or the state and so on this basis also it is clear that the civil society is committed to recognising religious freedom and may not 'direct or inhibit acts that are religious' (art. 3).

The Range of Religious Freedom

The range of religious freedom is derived from a further consideration of man's worth and dignity as a knowing, free being as well as of the nature of religion itself.

To seek the truth effectively as a human being, man must enjoy freedom of communication. It is only in association and exchange with others that he can arrive at some personal grasp of the truth. In this as in all other matters he is a social being (art. 4). His immunity from coercion then must be guaranteed for his social as well as his individual search for the truth, profession of it, living it and propagating it. Anything less would be subhuman. It would not allow him to function as the kind of knowing, free being that he is, one who must achieve knowledge and exercise freedom in some social way. Religious freedom then applies not only to his individual activities but to his social activities, to his association with others in religious activities. Religious societies or communities must enjoy immunity from coercion in the same way that the individual does if his freedom is to be a genuine one. And this applies to the whole range of what is called religious activity, whether corporative or individual.

The Declaration specifies at some length this range of activity (art. 4). It applies to profession and propagation of belief, to public worship, to international organisation and government, to communication with religious groups and authorities abroad, to establishment of institutions and possession of property necessary or useful to development of religious truth and living, to showing relevance of their beliefs for social life and so on. In the final draft the right of the parents in regard to the religious education of the children was included (art. 5).

The Limits of Religious Freedom

Religious freedom is a certain immunity from coercion which all men should enjoy. Yet like all freedoms it should be exercised responsibly. There is a moral obligation then on all men not to abuse this freedom by interfering with the equivalent rights of others by unfair methods of propaganda for instance, or by disrupting the social order necessary to men in exercising their rights. Just as all men have a responsibility to ensure religious liberty in society, so all men have a responsibility to ensure that it is not abused and so undermined. This applies particularly to the privileged ones in society, privileged through education or power—religious or civil. But it is a moral responsibility of all (art. 6).

It is in particular the responsibility of the civil authority to provide the legal guarantees within which the religious liberty of all may be co-ordinated and exercised. Religious liberty of itself is not granted by the state. It transcends or is superior to state power. Yet the state must guarantee it legally if it is to be effectively exercised. Similarly the state must protect society from certain offences against the necessary social order, even if they are done in the name of religious liberty. There are limits, then, to what may be done in the name of religious liberty (art. 7). There are first of all moral limits binding on all men. But some of them must be turned into legal limits upheld by the civil authority as a protection for a society of free men. On the Declaration's terms these limits are demanded by the need to protect the rights of all and settle conflicts, to maintain public peace and public morality (art. 7). These elements of the common welfare of society which the civil authority must uphold are collectively described in the document as 'public order'. Religious freedom should be guaranteed then by the civil authority within the limits of public order.

Such a statement cannot of itself settle the difficulties that may arise in practice. The Declaration gives some further guarantees. The limits may not be interpreted arbitrarily by government or used in a discriminating way against one or other religion. The government's action it is said, 'is to be controlled by juridical norms' (art. 7) which seems to mean by laws properly enacted and not administrative decisions of a government minister or the police for example. And the overriding principle is as much freedom as possible, as little restriction as necessary (art. 7).

The description of limits here is generally sound and in agreement, as we shall see, with other Christian statements as well as secular documents. But application in an actual situation can be very difficult, especially in regard to what is described as public morality. The genuine Christian tradition reflected in St Augustine and St Thomas, for example, has always been aware of this difficulty. It distinguished between private immoral acts such as telling a lie within the family and acts publicly immoral which affected the common welfare of civil society, such as perjury. Only acts publicly immoral in that sense could be outlawed as crimes or violations of public morality. But public morality itself could not be simply identified with full Christian morality and was related to the mores or beliefs and practices of particular communities at particular times. So some activities in themselves immoral and public might be legally permitted because of the community belief and practice. It is clear that some immoral practices such as child sacrifice and ritual prostitution would not be tolerated in the name of religious freedom. But there are a great many difficulties today in determining the actual level of public morality and what may or should be tolerated. In all this, frank discussions between the civil and religious leaders on the principles and practices involved and the foreseeable social consequences of change are very important. Legal acceptance of what has clearly evil consequences socially should not be granted at the whim of a minority. Yet mere head counting cannot be the decisive factor in legally permitting or disallowing some practice regarded as evil by the majority. It is in this area that the most delicate problems connected with religious freedom and freedom of conscience arise in Western countries.

The Declaration which opened so uncharacteristically for Church documents on this matter by noting and approving the common consciousness today of the need for religious freedom in private and public (art. 1) concludes by recognising that this 'freedom has already been declared to be a civil right in most constitutions, and it is solemnly recognised in international documents' (art. 15). Yet there are countries where there is no such recognition or it is a dead letter. The Council appeals to Catholics and to all men to ensure universal recognition in theory and in practice. By this Declaration it has given a valuable and necessary lead. The Roman Catholic Church gathered in Council has solemnly recognised each man's right to religious freedom in public as well as in private, socially as well as individually within the necessary limits of public order. It concludes a decade or more of hectic discussion amongst Catholic writers and thinkers by affirming the right so unambiguously.

The Declaration and the Council

But how central was the Declaration to the work of the Council? How far were the keen debates, the crises, the newspaper headlines related to the worth of a document very brief in itself? Or how far were they the outcome of personal interests and sensational reporting?

The aims of the Council as outlined by Pope John were renewal of the Church with a view to making a more effective approach to other Christians. This was more fully developed by Pope Paul in his speech to the second session calling for renewal based on increased self-knowledge with a view to dialogue with other Christians and the world at large. Where does the Declaration on Religious Liberty fit into these aims?

Self-Knowledge and Renewal

Most of the Council's sixteen documents concern directly the Church's self-examination and self-knowledge as a necessary means to revitalisation and renewal. *Ecclesia semper reformanda*, the Church always in need of reform, has become a catch-word today. And the reform can only proceed from increased understanding. The major documents here are undoubtedly the dogmatic Constitutions on the Church and on Divine Revelation and the Constitution on the Liturgy. Of these the Constitution on the Church is at once the most comprehensive and profound. And it is as developments of some points in these that the decrees dealing with the Church's internal life and mission should be understood.

The self-understanding of the Church and the practical consequences for reform which emerge from these documents can help us to see the Declaration in at least one conciliar perspective: that of self-understanding. God's communication of himself to mankind reached its climax in Christ, God the Son become man. Here is the source of revelation, revelation itself in the person and teaching, life, death and resurrection of the God-man. The Constitution on Revelation sees this fact as the dominating centre—God revealing himself to man, communicating himself to man out of love, asking for man's love in response. Christ is the sign and realisation of God's loving presence to man. And this sign-realisation is continued in the Church. The opening chapter of *Lumen Gentium* indicates this—it is headed 'The Mystery of the Church'. Mystery here is being used in its original sense which was the same as sacrament, a sign or outward indication that makes present a hidden and divine reality. The Church indicates and realises Christ's continuing presence in the world and so God's continuing presence to man inviting him. And this presence is in and through a people, a people freely called by God and freely answering him, a people who fully realise their sign and reality when, assembled with Christ about the altar, they are given a share in his own giving of himself to the Father for mankind on Calvary. The people become most properly God's people and that sign and realisation for mankind of his loving presence to all men through the eucharistic liturgy (*De Sacra Liturgia*).

With this vision of the Church as incorporating God's loving presence asking man's loving response, the Declaration of Religious Liberty harmonises perfectly. Indeed it would seem demanded by that vision. How else could the invitation be seen to be lovingly and freely offered? How else could the genuineness of the response be guaranteed? An over-juridical picture of the Church where the external organisation and its legal rights were central could obscure the freedom of the invitation and response. Vatican II's contribution to our understanding of the Church prevents this.

Relations with other Christians

The increased understanding and consequent reform were intended to promote our relationships with other Christians. The pain of disunity felt by Pope John and so many other Christians within and without the Roman Church had been one of the great motivating factors in the summoning and work of the Council. The tangible proof of this is most evident in the Decree on Ecumenism but in other ways great and small the unity theme had a decisive influence at the Council.

From the very first contacts between Roman Catholics and other Christians, the question of religious liberty had been a thorny one. Most other Christians believed up to very recently that the Roman Church was committed in principle to suppression of other religions where it was strong enough to effect this. And they felt they had practical confirmation of this in a country like Spain. It would be impossible to conduct genuine ecumenical conversations if this were true of course, and almost impossible to conduct them in an atmosphere where it was not clearly ruled out as untrue. The Secretariat for Promoting Christian Unity was well aware of this and had prepared a statement very early on which was subsequently introduced to the Council as the fifth chapter of the Decree on Ecumenism. Without some such statement ecumenical dialogue would not be possible. This was evident to any thinking Christian and was made explicit in articles in the journal of the World Council of Churches, the *Ecumenical Review,* and elsewhere.

The Council's own Decree on Ecumenism, adopted at the end of the third session, made anything less than a clear affirmation of religious liberty untenable. It accepts other Christians as brothers in Christ and their 'Communities' or 'Churches' as containing 'some, even very many of the most significant elements which together go to build up and give life to the Church itself' (Decree on Ecumenism, art. 3). They have much of the true Christian liturgy and the means of grace and so have their own 'significance and importance in the mystery of salvation' (art. 3). Indeed in the work of promoting unity which is said to be the task of all, common prayer and even public worship in certain circumstances, common study with mutual instruction and benefit as well as social co-operation are said to be the principal means (Decree, Chapter 2). Yet any and all of them would be unthinkable apart from the common recognition and guarantee of religious freedom.

In its brief statement on non-Christian religions the Council again adopts a position of recognising the good and truth of their teaching and morality and of respecting their persons and communities. This document gives special attention to the Jews, the historical and contemporary sign for the Christian of an intolerable intolerance developed from some religious roots.

The Church and the World

The Church in Council did not confine itself to Catholic or Christian domestic affairs. It was very aware of its existence for mankind, for the world and not as an end in itself. This comes through in great documents like *Lumen Gentium* but it was in the Constitution on the Church in the Modern World that these cares were fully revealed and developed.

Here the Church makes her own the joys and sorrows, achievements and frustrations of modern man. It is concerned with his dignity or value as a person, his family and community life, his need for freedom, justice, peace and love as previously summed up in Pope John's *Pacem in Terris*. And it desires to be of some service to him in pursuit of these. The approach is that of sympathetic understanding and humble service. Self-conscious of its role of revealing God to all men, the Church presents itself in the role of Christ the loving minister or servant with a measure of truth, an offer of co-operation and an assurance of love, but without any pretension to having ready-made answers for the many and involved human problems immediately facing mankind. It is a stance that shows a respect for human dignity and freedom in a way that demands religious freedom for all, even those of no religion or those who are anti-religious. Indeed its treatment of atheism and atheists, its sympathy for their difficulties, its admission of responsibility on the part of Christians also for the growth of unbelief and its offer of co-operation in tackling the problems of hunger, war and so on, shows how committed the Church is to this notion of religious freedom even for the irreligious.

However, the necessity and adequacy of the Declaration in speaking to all men of good will may be perhaps better assessed by comparing it with some important secular statements.

The first of these is the U.N. Declaration of Human Rights issued in 1948.

Article 18: 'Everyone has a right to freedom of thought, conscience and religion; this right includes freedom to change his religion or belief, and freedom, either alone or in community with others and in public or private, to manifest his religion or belief in teaching, practice, worship and observance.'

Whatever the religious, philosophical or other beliefs of the man who drafted this article, where the right to freedom is understood in the only way of interest to statesmen as an immunity from social coercion in believing, professing, changing one's religion, etc., it pretty well coincides with the position of Vatican II. The question of limits is not raised here as it is simply a general declaration.

The European Convention for the Protection of Human Rights is naturally more precise in its statement. Repeating Article 18 of the U.N. Declaration in Article 9, Paragraph 1, it goes on to define the limits in Paragraph 2: 'Freedom to manifest one's religion or beliefs shall be subject only to such limitations as are prescribed by law and are necessary in a democratic society in the interests of public safety, for the protection of public order, health or morals or for the protection of the rights and freedom of others.'

This closely resembles the limits laid down in the Declaration—only such as are necessary and prescribed by law for the public peace or safety, the protection of public morals and of the rights and freedom of others.

This Declaration was signed by members of the Council of Europe including Ireland.

Ireland could assent to Article 9 with a good conscience in view of Article 44 of its own Constitution which is without parallel in the fundamental law of a land so religiously homogeneous as Ireland was in 1937. The guarantee of religious freedom in Article 44 was a notable contribution in theory and practice in the evolution of Catholic thinking on the matter.

Conclusion

The religious freedom recognised in the Declaration is an immunity from all social coercion, open or hidden, in the matter of religion. It is a responsibility of all of us to recognise it, to uphold it and to exercise it justly. It has limits and may be abused. Legal measures help to define these limits and prevent public abuse. But in the long run the genuineness and value of our religious liberty depends not on the letter of the law but on the spirit of the responsible citizen and Christian.

II

Teaching Moral Theology Today

A GREAT deal has been said and written in recent years about the need for renewal in moral theology, the need to make it more biblical, dynamic, personal, Christ-centred, the need to integrate it into the other movements of renewal in the Church in Scripture, dogma, liturgy and ecumenism, and the need to integrate with the philosophical, psychological and sociological advances of our time. All this is very familiar stuff and I propose to take it as read. My only comment on it must be that by and large I accept the need for renewal in these ways and that I think it has received official approval in the Decree on Priestly Training which has emerged from Vatican II. After its insistence that theological disciplines should be renewed 'through a more living contact with the mystery of Christ and the history of salvation', the decree goes on to deal with moral theology in the following terms:

> Special care must be given to the perfecting of moral theology. Its scientific exposition, nourished more on the teaching of the Bible, should shed light on the loftiness of the calling of the faithful in Christ and the obligation that is theirs of bearing fruit in charity for the life of the world.

The call for a more biblical moral theology which studies the call or invitation to follow Christ and is expounded in terms of the necessary expressions of charity summarises much that has been said in the recent movement for renewal in moral theology. It is perhaps worth noting that while in the Constitution *De Sacra Liturgia*, article 16 makes a special demand on the professors of Scripture and of dogmatic, ascetical and pastoral theology to explain the relationship of their subject to the liturgy, it makes no such demand on the professors of moral theology. The developed understanding of moral theology suggested in the Decree on Priestly Training might well have made a difference here.

I am not concerned then with arguing for a renewal of moral theology, but with outlining a course in General or Fundamental Moral Theology, that section of moral theology described in the manuals as *De Principiis,* as an indication of what the renewal may bring.

PART I: INTRODUCTION TO GENERAL MORAL
THEOLOGY

To outline a course in general moral theology naturally presupposes a certain understanding of moral theology. What my understanding is will be very quickly evident.

Before embarking on a systematic exposition of the subject an introductory section helps to clarify the presuppositions as well as aims of the course and to give the student an understanding of how his study of moral theology fits into the rest of his study and into his life. The introduction may be divided into three chapters.

Chapter I is called The Meaning of Christian Moral Theology. It defines theology, Christian theology and moral theology, distinguishing it from and relating it to the other branches of theology, indeed all the other sciences which have a bearing on it, theological, philosophical and empirical. In particular it is necessary to stress the dependence of moral theology on Scripture as the standard account of revelation, its unity with dogmatic or doctrinal theology, its clear distinction from the moral science of ethics on the one hand and from the juridical study of canon law on the other. Moral theology is that part of the scientific study of the revelation made in Christ and carried out subject to the teaching authority of Christ now exercised in his Church, which studies man's free behaviour, his way of life. In so far as one may and should distinguish dogmatic and moral theology—the distinction is largely material and finally arbitrary—dogmatic theology confines itself to studying revelation as truth while moral theology handles that truth as a way of life, a norm of behaviour. Of course the truth is the life, and the truths discovered, defined and elaborated in dogmatic theology are taken up as sources of life and conditions of behaviour in moral theology.

Chapter II of the introductory section might be devoted to biblical moral theology. All theology must be biblical but there has grown up a biblical theology which is a systematic presentation of some of the ideas of revelation in the context and terms of the Bible alone. And it is important to introduce students at this stage to the Bible as the immediate source of their moral theology. (There are many helpful books here. For the New Testament Rudolf Schnackenburg's *The Moral Teaching of the New Testament,* Ceslas Spicq's *St Paul and Christian Living* and C. H. Dodd's *Gospel and Law* are perhaps the most accessible and helpful for students.)

In this chapter various methods may be followed. Some idea of the development between the Old and New Testaments might be given. A theme such as the kingdom in the New Testament could be traced in its importance for morality. The relation between liberty and law, Christian morality as a covenant morality, the Sermon on the Mount, the centrality of charity and its relation to the other virtues, any or some of these might be treated in strictly biblical terms. And however brief the treatment may have to be, as long as it gets the students reading the Bible as a source book for moral theology it will have achieved its purpose. In the systematic presentation there must be continual recourse to the Bible and biblical teaching for each particular section.

But some lectures exclusively on biblical themes at the very beginning of the course are very helpful.

In the third and final chapter in the introductory section the history of moral theology should be treated. This is not to be thought of as of exclusively academic interest or as not sufficiently 'pastoral'. The use or abuse of the word 'pastoral' is one of the less satisfactory features of the present interest in seminary and theological renewal. Good theology, which means rigorously scientific theology, the systematic attempt to understand the Christian message in terms intelligible and relevant to the men of today, is necessarily pastoral. It is the only theology that is, because it is the only theology that is genuine. What was criticised in the past as non-pastoral was, where the criticism was justified, simply bad theology. Certain studies in both historical and speculative theology may be unsuited to the needs of a particular audience, such as seminarians, but even these, if they are genuine studies, will have pastoral implications in clearing the way for that understanding of the Christian message in the modern world which all ultimately require.

That their theology be truly pastoral, students must understand its historical dimension. Theology is rooted in history. In a real sense it is history—the history of the community's questioning of and reflection on the revelation made in Christ. The failure to grasp this has frequently presented theologians and the pastors whom they serve with unnecessary dilemmas. The achievements of Vatican II and the painful struggle in search of them are reminders of that. But the conciliar documents and the theological developments endorsed by them are in danger of being taken out of their historical context as so many other documents and developments have been in the past.

The historical perspective in theology must be seen in all sections of it but it is very helpful for students to have some special treatment of it here and precisely in reference to moral theology. This may be done by outlining the development of moral theology, its place in general theology up to and including scholastic times, and then its gradual emergence and even separation from Scripture and dogmatic theology as a distinct theological science. An analysis in their historical context of some of the contributory influences such as the *Summae Confessariorum* and their forerunners in the Irish Penitentials, the collections of Canon Law, the nominalist and voluntarist theologians of the first manuals, the probabilist controversies and the later attempts at renewal, both neo-scholastic and biblical, would make the present transitional stage in its absolutes and relativities more intelligible and acceptable. Alternatively, tracing the historical development and expression of a particular moral value would be a very useful exercise in understanding the historical dimension.

PART II: SYSTEMATIC MORAL THEOLOGY

Chapter One: The Structure of Moral Theology

Systematic moral theology begins with the structure of moral theology. If moral theology is defined as a study of the Christian life, a study of the revelation made in Christ as prescribing how man ought to live, the structure of moral theology arises out of the structure of revelation. Revelation is God's communication of himself to man, not simply communication by image and reflection which creation constitutes, but the communication of himself as he is in himself. This communication is summed up in Christ, for whose coming all preceding revelation was merely a preparation. The point of God's self-communication, however, was not the imparting of information but the initiation of a relationship. God loved man and gave himself to man, communicated himself to him that man might love God in return, might enter into a personal relationship of love with him. The whole history of the divine interventions in human history follows the *donum-mandatum* pattern, God's gift of himself to man calling for man's response. The structure of revelation is that of a relationship initiated by God—it is an invitation-response structure. This structure enters into

o

God's total relationship with the human race throughout time. It is well to stress that it was to the race or human community as a whole that he communicated himself but he has in this a personal relationship with each individual human person. And the invitation-response structure applies to this relationship in its totality as well as to each period and area of his life and finally to each individual situation in which man has to make a decision. It is necessary then to allow this invitation-response structure to emerge very clearly in the organisation of general moral theology and of the special sections so that priests and all Christians may be more aware of the reality of their situation.

The structure itself must be analysed further in the light of the Christian revelation. The divine self-communication achieves its full, indeed its uniquely proper expression in Christ. In Christ too man's response is realised to the full. There are then three focal points in this structure, God, man, and the God-man Christ. And it is about these three points that the course in general moral theology is organised. The basically unifying relationship between God and man is analysed in terms of these three points to give a complete account of the basic principles governing human behaviour as laid down by the Christian revelation, the basic principles of Christian moral theology.

Chapter Two: God as Source of Invitation and Term of Response

The section dealing with the first focal point, God, might, of course, be expanded to include not only the whole of this course but the whole of theology. Divisions here as elsewhere in theology are somewhat artificial. And it is important for students to realise this. Theology is the one study of God as he has revealed himself. And as he has revealed himself to man, he is at once the source of invitation to man and the term of his response.

Here moral theology presupposes the dogmatic treatment of God as he has revealed himself and applies the dogmatic truths to a discussion of Christian living. And the God who is relevant to Christian living is not the God of the philosophers, of creation, but primarily of the theologians, of revelation. There is no contradiction between the absolute being, first cause, unmoved mover of the philosophers, who is manifested in creation and the God of theology and revelation. But it is precisely as he has revealed himself in revelation, as he is in fact in himself, that he is source of invitation and term of response. For the invitation and response arise out of the communication of himself as he is himself, as we find him in revelation, and not as he is imaged and reflected in creation. That he is a personal, loving and relational being determines the invitation and response. His interventions are the result of his free, personal initiative in seeking a love-relationship with man and not the mechanical working out of some impersonal design. More specifically, he meets man finally and fully in Christ as a three-personal God. The Trinity is known to man through the role of the three persons in the God-man relationship—initiated by the Father, accomplished in and through the Son and extended to all mankind by the gift of the Spirit. The invitation-response structure of the God-man relationship and of moral theology has a trinitarian character. It is here that the relevance and indeed centrality of the doctrine of the Trinity in Christianity becomes apparent, so that it is no longer simply a theological luxury of little importance for daily living. And in this context it makes more sense to speak of special personal relations with each of the three divine persons, because by this relationship man is no longer simply *ad extra,* but in a real sense *ad intra,* admitted to sharing the inner trinitarian life. And this inner trinitarian life is above all a life of love.

The God who is the source of invitation and term of response is this triune God who has gradually manifested himself in history in his self-communication to man, thereby drawing man into a personal relationship at the divine level.

The terminus or end to which man is drawn is this full

sharing in the divine life. At this stage it is necessary to explain the concepts of *terminus, finis,* end, as applying to the Creator and his creation, to the creature and his activity. And the basic Thomistic analysis of the last end as the ultimate determinant of human behaviour can be integrated into the invitation-response approach in a dynamic and personalist manner. Every good human response is partial achieving of that final destiny. It is a fuller sharing by man in the inner trinitarian life, a further step in the manifestation and realisation of the divine self-communication in the world, of the divine love in the world.

Chapter Three: Man as Term of Invitation and Source of Response

The first point to be made about man as term of invitation and source of response is that he is a creature. This may seem too obvious to be worth stressing. Yet the distinction between creature and Creator is a central mystery of reality and the necessary basis to the Creator-creature, God-man relationship. In preserving man's creatureliness we preserve the possibility of a genuine God-man relationship.

He is of course a creature of a particular kind, with particular endowments. He is a spiritual creature, created in the image of God with all that implies. He can know and understand, a necessary presupposition to reading the divine invitation. He can freely choose and so respond. In accordance with his spiritual character, he can take possession of himself, the source of his autonomy, and so commit or entrust himself by entering a relationship. He is a relational being. He can love.

All this man does as a spiritual-material being. He is a single unified being, part of the physical material world, subject to its laws, yet emerging from it and making it subject to himself. This physical aspect of man affects him very directly in his role as a term of the divine invitation. It is only through media that are physical as well as spiritual that he can receive the invitation—through physical persons, words and deeds. And it is only through the use of his bodily organs that he can in human fashion respond.

As a creature and a physical creature, man exists in time. He is subject to change and development. It is only gradually that he develops the capacity of understanding, with the growth and use of the necessary physical organs. It is only gradually that he acquires physical, emotional and intellectual possession of himself so that he can respond and love. And this development never ceases, although there may be critical stages in it as when he acquires that first level of understanding traditionally known as the 'use of reason', and at the onset of the confusion of adolescence, and at the beginning of adult maturity.

Man's capacity to understand the divine invitation and to respond to it has a history. Man is a historical being. His understanding and response should have this dynamic, historical quality as achievements of somebody on the way, a pilgrim. So the individual human act must be set in the context of the person's development and judged on whether it contributes to his advance towards God or away from him. Some individuals (i.e. children mentally retarded) will not have reached that stage which would enable them to take a decisive step forward or backward (mortal sin). And while he is in this pilgrim state, because of his historical character, man cannot commit himself at one moment so definitively and exhaustively to God or away from him that no further change is possible. He never possesses the fullness of his being at any one moment of his history.

Man as the recipient of the divine invitation and source of response is a community being. It was to the human community that the invitation was initially given. And it is in the history of human community that it was gradually manifested and achieved. It is through the community that the invitation is extended to the individual. He comes into being community-wise in the family. He grows and develops through sharing the community-life and community-goods, physical and spiritual. Without participating in the community-life at least for a time, he would not develop as a human being—a being who is not simply absorbed by the community. He achieves in community his own identity and autonomy. This concept of the person-in-community needs emphasising in face of an extreme individualism on the one hand (not without influence in some presentations of Catholic moral theology) and an extreme collectivism on the other. It is with the person-in-community that the divine invitation reaches its ultimate term. It is both a community and personal invitation. And the true personal response will be in and through the community.

As a member of a historical community man is a cultural being. He is formed or at least influenced by the prevailing modes of thought, language, social organisation, economic state of development and all the other factors which make up the concrete life of this particular community at this particular time. (He should in turn of course contribute to and influence this way of life.) His openness to the divine invitation will be culturally conditioned by the historical life of the community to which he belongs and so will his response.

Finally, it should be mentioned that he receives the divine invitation as a sexual being, male or female. The implications of this cannot be developed very fully in general moral theology but they should be kept in mind in discussing the concrete understanding of the invitation by a particular individual and his or her capacity to respond. In history the respective roles of male and female and so their opportunities of understanding and response have been culturally conditioned to a large extent.

It is to man as a spiritual-material, historical and community being that the invitation is addressed. It is through his knowing, free activity that he is able to respond. Such activity, based on his understanding of the invitation, of the good in the concrete situation, and the result of his free choice, is his way of seeking his final destiny. He is invited to respond knowingly and freely. Such knowing, free activity is called (properly) human activity or responsible activity—activity which has this capacity for response or activity for which a man may be expected to account or to answer. Both these ideas, radically the same, are contained in the notion of responsible activity.

It will be responsible then in so far as it is knowing, free activity, in so far as a man knows what he is doing and is free to do it. By such activity a man engages himself, commits himself, identifies himself with that which he has chosen.

The capacity to know and to choose in that way is radically but not effectively given to man at birth. He must gradually and sometimes painfully acquire it, and his acquisition of it will be conditioned by his own material nature, the community in which he develops and the historical stage of development he has reached. It will always be limited but should be in the process of developing. However, it may be fixated at some relatively low level due to some material, psychological, social or spiritual defect. The factors reducing responsibility must be considered here.

Deliberate refusal to know is of course a responsible attitude in itself. Failure to respond to an invitation which one refuses explicitly or implicitly to read is in fact culpable failure. But there are many other factors personal and social which may prevent the correct understanding of the invitation or prevent the person from freely performing that which he knows he should do.

These factors include the classic impediments to voluntariety treated in the manuals following St Thomas. They must, however, be set in the modern context of our fuller understanding of man, especially of the psychological and social factors which qualify or diminish his understanding and freedom. So the findings of modern psychology and psychiatry on mental handicap and mental illness must be considered in relation to personal responsibility as also must the social and cultural factors which so heavily condition a man's understanding and freedom but which he may be called on to overcome or transform in association with others who gradually perceive the need. The final test, however, is how far was a man aware of what he was doing and how far was he free to do it. And it should be remembered that there are some actions of which a man is well aware but over which he has no control, for example, compulsive drinking in alcoholism.

The humanity (knowledge and freedom) of the action determines its response-capacity. But how far it is a 'yes' or 'no' response, an acceptance or rejection of the invitation, determines its morality. Morality is perhaps best understood in this context as a quality of direction inherent in the human act, making it a 'yes' or 'no' response. An action which says 'yes' to the invitation is a good action, an action which says 'no' is a bad action.

There is a basic human capacity to distinguish the 'yes' and 'no' responses, moral good and evil, but it has a history for the race, for the particular community and for the individual human being. Some account of that history enables students to have a richer and more refined understanding of morality and its role in their own lives and in the lives of others. The distinction between objective and subjective morality arises naturally in this setting.

As a 'yes' or 'no' response, the morality of the action necessarily involves the person. It is he who is identified by his action with the acceptance or rejection. And the action must never be separated from the person. Yet it is necessary to analyse it further to see its component parts. This may be a material analysis of object or *finis operis*, that end or term to which the action of itself tends, and motive or *finis operantis*, that end or term to which it is referred by the agent. These are the traditional *fontes moralitatis*, the sources of the morality of the action, so that both object and motive must be good if the action is to be good. If either is bad, the total action is bad because the agent had identified himself with the evil. Here too is the place to discuss the act of double effect.

There are other possible analyses of human activity. As a material, historical being, man does not immediately engage himself in an activity in a full human way. Many of his actions will not express him in a way that would identify him with an acceptance or rejection of the divine invitation. There are actions which are trivial or slight. These may be in the 'yes' direction or the 'no' direction. There are 'venial' good actions as well as 'venial' bad actions. And the serious, critical good or bad actions have a certain history, they need some time (on occasion very brief perhaps) in which to engage the person fully. Such critical actions are perhaps less frequent than is sometimes believed, but this applies equally to good and bad actions. And it is only through critical good actions that a man responds effectively to the divine invitation and that he can return after rejecting the invitation earlier.

In all this the emphasis has been on man. Yet the very fact of the invitation changes him. By speaking to man, by entering into a relationship with him, God changed him, raised him to the divine level. He did not destroy his humanity. But from the very beginning that humanity has existed in a supernatural order. He is still a spiritual-material, historical, community and sexual being. The direction of his response is the same. But the level at which he is responding is not merely human but divine. And the relationship itself has a history. Man from the beginning has disrupted that relationship, has refused the invitation. He is fallen man. Yet God has persisted in loving him. He has constantly renewed the relationship. He has established it permanently in becoming man and so provided the way of reconciliation or redemption for all men.

The man who is term of invitation and source of response is fallen and redeemed man. While the response is genuinely human, it is also truly divine. Through his association with the God-man Christ, who is the full expression of the Father's invitation and each man's way of response, he receives the capacity for such a human-divine response.

Chapter Four: Christ as Bearer of Invitation and Manner of Response

Chapter four on Christ as Bearer of Invitation and Manner of Response, is the heart of the course on General Moral Theology, but as I have discussed it in detail elsewhere,[1] I will deal with it briefly here.

In Christ the self-communication of God to man reached the climax. The response of man to God was fully realised. It is only by the power and after the manner of Christ that any man can come to the Father. He forms the norm or standard of morality, the test of the direction of man's response. This may be explored in the New Testament in terms of following and imitating Christ, of sharing his life and destiny not simply by external association but by internal transformation and finally in terms of participating in his divine human-being as the Son of God made man. It is to be sons (and daughters) of the Father that mankind is invited. The relationship they must live out is that of sonship, of sharing in the divine life at the level of the Son. So the *esse filiationis divinae* which they share with the man Christ determines their *agere*. And this sonship of the Father is at the same time a brotherhood of one another. So the internal law of their being can be summarised in the two great precepts of charity, which are really one. The law is primarily internal and unwritten, only secondarily written.[2] From the further analysis of this moral norm or law that is Christ it can be seen that it is a community reality. The building of the human community, of the brotherhood of man through the sonship of the Father in Christ provides another aspect of Christ as norm of morality. It is the one norm for all men. They have all the same destiny to be achieved in the same way. But its manifestations and realisations have a history. It is a historical reality. There is a definite historical development in the history of mankind as in the history of the individual of what is basically the one reality.

And this one reality has genuine human and divine

dimensions. It is a single reality but materially composed of the human and the divine. For Christ is both human and divine. The only way the divine can enter man's world is through the human. The only way man can be truly human is as bearer of the divine. These two dimensions in the norm of morality can be distinguished but not separated. And that aspect of the norm enshrined in the humanity, in the created spiritual-material, historical, community and sexual part of the one reality, may be taken abstractly on its own and described as natural moral law or the moral directions arising from man's human nature which are fully respected in the existing human-divine order. Natural law may not be the happiest term for this but it is here that a discussion of this reality or part of reality finds its place. The material elements of the one reality, which indicate and realise the divine element, are even less happily described as divine positive law. Together, however, they form the one reality, man's way of life summed up in Christ.

The divine invitation may not be exhaustively written down in precepts of natural law and divine positive law. And the invitation is not in the concrete circumstances always simply an application or realisation of *essential* obligations which are common to all men and to all Christians, arising from their *essence* as men called to be sons of the Father. It will never contradict these essential obligations but it may go beyond them in existential obligations proper to this person in this particular situation. In a person-to-person relationship such demands are only to be expected. And an ethic of love, which the ethic of sonship is, is necessarily creative and goes beyond the mechanical realisation of essential requirements. When we have done that which we ought, we are unprofitable servants.

To conclude this chapter it is necessary to deal with man's social life and its organisation by human law. This law which man needs for effective social living derives from man's God-given social character and has its place in the community of the faithful, in the Church and in the political organisation of mankind in the state. It should be respected and observed as the way of seeking a fuller Christian and human life which is only possible in community but it must be carefully distinguished from the direct *personal* requirements of the divine invitation itself as expressed in Christ.

Chapters Five and Six: Conscience: Sin

In chapter five the personal understanding of the divine invitation in the individual situation is discussed. This understanding on which man bases his here-and-now response is called conscience. A biblical approach provides the correct background for a more systematic study of conscience as man's reading of the invitation and of his obligation to respond in accordance with that reading, to follow his conscience. The problems of the true and false conscience, the certain and doubtful, the manifestive and constitutive, may be most fruitfully discussed in the setting of man's obligation to obtain a true reading of the divine invitation as far as he can and to respond to it as far as he knows it. Again the spiritual-material, historical and community character of man as well as the historical and community character of revelation or the invitation will be of importance. It is in community, properly in the Christian community, but always in some human community that man will attempt to discover the good to be done or evil avoided. And his capacity to do this develops in history and is conditioned by material and social factors.

Here too it will be important to discuss alternative theories of conscience and morality, the conditioned reflex of the behaviourists, the super-ego of the Freudians, the autonomous conscience of the situationists, etc., and to see the value as well as the deficiencies of these various attempts to explain a basic human phenomenon.

The sixth and last chapter of this systematic presentation of General Moral Theology discusses the fact of man's failure, knowing and free failure, to say 'yes' to the divine invitation, the fact of sin. Again a biblical introduction gives the student an immense awareness of the centrality of sin in the story of the God-man relationship as well as an appreciation of its essential characteristics.

Without here presenting a developed treatment of sin, I merely draw attention to some interesting and neglected points.

As it is basically a refusal of the divine invitation, it is a form of self-centredness, of turning in on oneself and refusing to open to God and the neighbour. It is also a refusal of light, an unwillingness to read the divine invitation, to know the one true God, to enter into a relationship with him. The sinner is a man who creates and worships false gods. It is at the same time a refusal to open up to the neighbour. As sonship of the Father and brotherhood of men are the same reality, a refusal of one is a refusal of the other. It is a community or rather an anti-community reality.

And it is a historical reality, existing and persevering in the history of the human community. As a historical reality it demands time. A radical refusal by man of the divine invitation only emerges after some time in what has already been described as a critical action. This history of slowly receding from God, of gradually becoming self-centred by 'contemning the small things' will sooner or later, unless there is a change of direction, culminate in such a critical action or rejection of God. For that you need awareness or understanding plus consent or commitment to a matter of such importance that the person is totally absorbed to the exclusion of God. Where this total absorption is not achieved, and so God is not completely excluded, through lack of awareness, lack of consent or the triviality of the matter there is venial sin. The basic relationship with God survives venial sin, although it is weakened by it, particularly by continuous and deliberate venial sin. The relationship is destroyed by mortal sin and can only be repaired by *metanoia,* total conversion, a critical action of return under the influence of God's loving attraction or grace.

CONCLUSION

In the three chapters of the introductory section and the six chapters of the systematic outlined here, I attempt to present a course in General Moral Theology. The basic invitation-response structure centred about God, man and Christ (with its trinitarian character), the development of Christ as norm and some understanding of God in his self-revelation and of man's spiritual-material, historical-community response (in the context of sin and redemption) constitute the basic elements of the discussion. Further study and understanding of these elements may yet provide a satisfactory course in general moral theology.

Notes

THE NATURAL LAW AND THE LAW OF CHRIST

[1]See my 'Moral theology: the need for renewal' in *Moral Theology Renewed: Papers of the Maynooth Union Summer School* 1964, ed. E. McDonagh, Dublin 1965.

[2]Cf. D. H. Dodd, *Gospel and Law*, Cambridge 1957.

[3]See B. Schüller, *Gesetz und Freiheit*, Düsseldorf 1966.

[4]See F. Böckle, *Das Naturrecht im Disput*, Düsseldorf 1966, 127ff.

[5]See also chapter 5, 'Penance and Charity'.

[6]See K. Rahner, 'Das "Gebot" der Liebe unter den anderen Geboten' *Schriften zur Theologie V*, Einsiedeln 1962, 494–517 (E. tr. *Theological Investigations V*, London 1966).

[7]This I have more fully developed in the following chapter.

[8]For moral theology one of the most important themes of contemporary theology is the eschatological orientation of Christian life. Cf. J. Moltmann, *Theologie der Hoffnung*, Munich 1966; J. B. Metz, *Zur Theologie der Welt*, Mainz-Munich 1968.

[9]*Gal.* 6:2; it became common usuage in the current renewal of moral theology with the publication in 1954 of B. Haring, *Das Gesetz Christi*, Freiburg i. Br., 8th ed. 1967.

[10]*S. theol.* I, II. 106, 1.

[11]*Ibid.*

[12]See J. Fuchs, *Moral und Moraltheologie nach dem Konzil*, Freiburg i. Br. 1967, 94 ff.

[13]See F. Böckle, *op. cit.*, 127ff.

[14]This is argued very effectively, although in different terms, by B. Schüller, *Wie weit Kann die Moraltheologie das Naturrecht entbehren?* Lebendiges Zeugnis 1965, 41–65.

[51]See F. Böckle, *op. cit.*, 127 ff.; J. Fuchs, *Lex Naturae*, Dusseldorf 1955, 13ff.

THE PRIMACY OF CHARITY

[1]Cf. M. Buber, *I and Thou*, Edinburgh 1937.

[2]Cf. E. Fromm, *The Art of Loving*, London 1962, 25–6.

[3]Cf. *S. theol.* I, II, q. 26, a. 4 etc.

[4]C. S. Lewis, *The Four Loves*, London 1960.

[5]London 1951.

[6]'Amans fit extra se in amatum translatus.'

[7]V. Warnach, *Agape: Liebe als Grundmotiv der neutestamentlichen Theologie*, Düsseldorf 1951, 462ff.

[8]For this relationship between Christian love and resurrection cf. Warnach, *op. cit.* 371ff.

[9]As Spicq points out (*Agape in the New Testament* 1, London 1963, 11) one must distinguish between *agapan* and *philein*, which latter, as the love of friendship, implies some affection and warmth of feeling. Yet the full human realisation of *agape* is incompatible with emotional dislike or resentment.

[10]Cf. *S. theol.* I, II, q. 62; II, II, q. 23.

[11]*S. theol.* II, II, q. 23, a. 8c.

[12]See *Denz. Schön.* 2181 ff.; 2201ff.

[13]Cf. J. A. T. Robinson, *Honest to God*, London 1963, 118; D. A. Williams, 'Theology and Self-Awareness' in A. Vidler (ed.), *Soundings*, Cambridge 1962, 81.

[14]Robinson, *op. cit.*; *id., Christian Morals Today*, London 1964.

[15]*No New Morality*, London 1964.

[16]H. McCabe, 'The Cartesian Basis of the New Morality', *Blackfriars*, May, 1964, 194ff.

[17]'And he said "What comes out of a man is what defiles a man. For from within, out of the heart of man come evil thoughts, fornication, theft, murder, adultery, coveting, wickedness, deceit, licentiousness, envy, slander, pride, foolishness. All these evil things come from within and they defile a man." ' (*Mark* 7:20–23.)

[18]Cf. I *Cor.* 13: *S. theol.* II, II, q. 23, a. 7c. 'Nulla vera virtus potest esse sine caritate.'

[19]*S. theol.* II, II, q. 23, a. 7, c.

[20]*S. theol.* II, II, q. 23, a. 8, c.

[21]*Ibid.*

[22]*The Primacy of Charity in Moral Theology*, London 1959.

[23]Cf. *De Virt.* 2, 3c. 'Caritas est motor omnium virtutum.'

[24]Gillemann, *op. cit.*, 35.

[25]'Das "Gebot" der Liebe unter der anderen Geboten', *Schriften zur Theologie* V, Einsiedeln 1962, 494–517 (E. tr. *Theological Investigations* V, London 1966,

[26]*Loc. cit.*, 507ff.

ETHICAL PROBLEMS OF ABORTION

Abbreviations

CSEL Corpus Scriptorum Ecclesiastorum Latinorum.

DS Denzinger/Schönetzer Enchiridion.

DTC Dictionnaire de Théologie Catholique.

PG Patrologia Greca.

S. theol. Thomas Aquinas, *Summa Theologica*.

[1]Paper read to the International Colloquium on Sexology, Louvain, May 1968.

[2]English translation published by Catholic Truth Society, London, cf. par· 62–66.

[3]Cf. English translation (C.T.S. London), 6–8.

[4]Abbott-Gallagher, *Documents of Vatican II*, London 1966, 255.

[5]Cf. McFadden, *Medical Ethics*, Philadelphia 1955, 161 ff. or any standard medical ethics textbook or moral theology manual.

[6]*The Lambeth Conference 1958*, London 1958, 2, 148.

[7]*Op. cit.*, 1, 23.

[8]Quoted in Robert F. Drinan, 'Contemporary Protestant Thinking', *America*, 117/24, 9 Dec. 1967, 713.

[9]G. Hornig, *Schwangerschaftsunterbrechung*, Gutersloh 1967, Anhang A. 49.

[10]This work was published posthumously in 1949. The English translation quoted was published by the Fontana Library, London 1964.

[11]Cf. Hornig, *op. cit.*, 20; M. Vogler, 'Schwangerschaftsunterbrechung in der Sicht der heutigen protestantischen', *Theologie und Glaube*, 52 (1962), 462ff.

[12]K. Barth, *Church Dogmatics*, III/4, Edinburgh 1961, 415ff.

[13]A. De Quervain, *Ethik, II*, Zurich 1953, 213ff.

[14]H. van Oyen, *Ethik, II*, Basle 1958, 368.

[15]N. Soe, *Ethik*, Munich 1957, 202.

[16]H. G. Fritzsche, *Evangelische Ethik*, Berlin 1963, 127f.

[17]H. Thielicke, *Theologische Ethik, II*, Tübingen 1964, 749ff.; *Sex-Ethik der Geschlechtlichkeit*, Tübingen 1966, 243ff.

[18]W. Trillhaas, *Ethik*, Berlin 1965, 195.

[19]K. Janssen, 'Die Unterbrechung der aufgezwungener Schwangerschaft als theologisches und rechtliches Problem', *Zeitschrift für Evangelische Ethik*, 1960, 65ff.

[20]Cf. Hornig, *loc. cit.*, Vogler, *loc. cit.*, Janssen, *loc. cit.*

[21]J. Fletcher, *Situation Ethics*, London 1966, 37–9.

[22]P. Ramsey, 'The Sanctity of Life', *The Dublin Review*, Spring 1967, 3ff. A similar stance is taken by Lutheran John Neuhaus, 'The Dangerous Assumptions', *Commonweal*, LXXXVI/15, 30 June 1967, 408ff. A more liberal but very thoughtful attitude is expressed by the Professor of Christian Ethics at Yale University, James Gustafson, 'A Christian Approach to the Ethics of Abortion', *The Dublin Review*, Winter 1967–68, 346ff.

[23]*Abortion*, 61.

[24]Cf. note 4 above.

[25]Cf. *Herder Korrespondenz*, 22/3, Marz 1968, 132–3.

[26]R. McCormick, 'Abortion: Aspects of the Moral Question', *America* 117/24, 9 Dec. 1967, 716ff.

[27]*Lehrbuch der Moraltheologie*, Freiburg 1878, 491ff.

[28]DS 3258; 3298; 3337; 3358.

[29]I am much indebted to Professor John T. Noonan's account in his recent historical study, 'The Catholic Church and Abortion', *The Dublin Review*, Winter 1967–68, 300ff.

[30]*Didache* ii, 2: 'You shall not kill. You shall not commit adultery. You shall not corrupt boys. You shall not make magic. You shall not practise medicine (*pharmakeia*). You shall not slay the child by abortions (*phthora*). You shall not kill what is generated. You shall not desire your neighbour's wife.'

[31]*Epistle of Barnabas*, xix, 5.

[32]Athenagoras, *Embassy for the Christians*, PG, 6.919.

[33]Minucius Felix, *Octavius*, CSEL, 2.43.

[34]Tertullian, *Apologeticum ad nationes*, 1.15.

[35]Clement, *Pedagogus*, 2.10.96.1.

[36]Cyprian, *Epistle*, 52, CSEL, 3.619.

[37]Can. 53, Mansi, 2.16.

[38]Can. 21, Mansi, 2.519.

[39]Jerome, *Epistle*, 22, to Eustochium, 13, CSEL, 54.160-1.

[40]Augustine, *De nuptiis et concupiscentia*, 1.15.17, CSEL, 42.229–30.

[41]Chrysostom, *Homily 24 on the Epistle to the Romans*, PG 626–7.

[42]Basil, *Letters*, PG, 32.672.

[43]Cf. *Epistle of Barnabas*, loc. cit.

[44]Cf. *Didache*, loc. cit.

[45]*Ibid.*

[46]*Didache, Ep. of Barnabas*, Minucius Felix, Tertullian.

[47]Cf. Jerome, Augustine, *loc. cit.*

[48]Noonan, *art. cit.* 313 ff.

[49]J. T. Noonan, *Contraception*, Cambridge 1965, 164.

[50]Gratian, *Decretum*, 2.32.2.7.

[51]*S. theol.*, 2.2.64. 8 ad 2.

[52]Gregory IX, *Dec.*, 5.12.20.

[53]Cf. *S. theol.*, 2–2, 64–7.

[54]Noonan, *art. cit.*, 319.

[55]See John of Naples, *Quadlibeta*; cf. Noonan, *art. cit.*, 321.

[56]Antoninus, *Summa Sacrae Theologiae*, Venice 1581, 3.7.2.

[57]Sylvester Da Prieras, *Summa summarum que sylvestrina dictur:*, 1518; Noonan, *loc. cit.*

[58]Thomas Sanchez, *De sancto matrimonii sacramento*, Venice 1737.

[59]Lessius, *De justitia et jure*, Lyons 1653, 2.9.2.58.

[60]Cf. Noonan, *art. cit.*, 325.

[61]Alphonsus Liguori, *Theologia Moralis, Opera Omnia*, Bk 3, n. 394, ed. L. Gaude, 1950.

[62]Noonan, *art. cit.*, 326ff.

[63]DS 2134.

[64]DS 2135.

[65]Cf. Noonan, *art. cit.*, 328.

[66]*Ibid.*

[67]*Ibid.*

[68]Noonan, *art. cit.*, 330.

[69]This is taken from an article by Thomas L. Hayes, biophysicist at the University of California at Berkeley, 'Abortion: A Biological View', *Commonweal*, LXXXV/23, 17 March 1967, 677.

[70]D. Mercier, *La psychologie*, III, Louvain 1899, 540ff.: cf. DTC 5, 1305ff.

[71]Cf. Noonan, *art. cit.*, 328ff.

[72]Donceel is referred to by McCormack, *art. cit.* and by Wassmer, cf. note 73 below.

[73]T. Wassmer, 'Abortion: Questions about Questions', *Commonweal*, LXXXVI/15, 30 June 1967, 417ff.

[74]*Abortion*, 29.

[75]J. J. Stamm and M. E. Andrew, *The Ten Commandments in Recent Research*, London 1967, 99; cf. H. van Oyen, *Ethik des Alten Testaments*, Gutersloh 1967, 120ff.; J. J. Stamm, 'Sprachliche Erwägungen zum Gebot "Du sollst nicht toten",' *Theologische Zeitschrift*, 1945, 81–90.

[76]Van Oyen, *loc. cit.*

[77]*Matt.* 5:21; 19:18; *Mark* 10:19; *Luke* 18:20. Murder is included in many catalogues of sins: *Matt.* 15:19; *Mark* 7:21; *Rom.* 1:29; *Gal.* 5:21 (some authorities); 1 *Tim.* 1:19; 1 *Pet.* 4:15; *Apoc.* 9:21; 21:8; 22:15.

[78]Cf. B. Schöpf, *Das Totungsrecht bei den fruhchristlichen Schriftstellern bis zur Zeit Konstantins*, Regensburg 1958.

[79]K. Barth, *Church Dogmatics*, III/4, 432.

[80]*Op. cit.*, 437ff.; 450ff.

[81]Cf. W. Conway, 'The Act of Two Effects', *Irish Theological Quarterly*, XVIII/2, April 1951, 125ff.

[82]Cf. C. B. Daly, *Morals, Law and Life*, Dublin 1962.

[83]Cf. E. D'Arcy, *Human Acts*, Oxford 1963.

[84]Cf. McFadden, *op. cit.*, 236 ff.

[85]Ramsey, *art. cit.*

[86]*Ibid.*

[87]McCormack, *art. cit.*

[88]J. Pleasants, 'A Morality of Consequences', *Commonweal*, LXXXVI, 414.

[89]The way discussion has developed among non-Roman theologians is some evidence of this. The proposed and actual changes in legislation reveal how small a part danger of death cases play in all this if they are taken by themselves and not used as a way of introducing the other cases.

[90]*Abortion*, 34.

[91]N. St John Stevas, 'Abortion and the Law', *The Dublin Review*, Winter, 1967–68, 276.

[92]*Abortion*, 34.

[93]Cf. *Herder Korrespondenz, loc. cit.*

[94]Cf. A. Hellegers, 'Law and the Common G o od', *Commonweal*, LXXXVI/15 30 June 1967, 420.

[95]*Abortion*, 43.

[96]Cf. Hornig, *op. cit.*; Janssen, *art. cit.*

TEACHING MORAL THEOLOGY TODAY

[1]Cf. my article 'Moral Theology Renewed' in *Irish Eccl. Rec.*, December 1965, also contributions to Maynooth Union Summer School book, *Moral Theology Renewed*, Dublin 1965. The topic is also dealt with in Chapter 2 above.

[2]*S. theol.* Ia, IIae, q. 106.